# PROCEEDINGS OF HOLINESS CONFERENCES

Cincinnati
November 26th, 1877

New York
December 17th, 1877

*Garland Publishing, Inc.*
*New York & London*
*1985*

For a complete list of the titles in this series
see the final pages of this volume.

This facsimile has been made from a copy in
the Boston Public Library.

Library of Congress Cataloging-in-Publication Data

Holiness Conferences (1877 : Cincinnati, Ohio
and New York, N.Y.)
*PROCEEDINGS OF HOLINESS CONFERENCES.*

("The Higher Christian life")
Reprint. Originally published: Philadelphia :
National Pub. Association for the
Promotion of Holiness, 1878.
1. Holiness churches—Congresses.  I. Title.  II. Series.
BX7990.H6H58  1877      289.9      85-16193
ISBN 0-8240-6438-0 (alk. paper)

The volumes in this series are printed on
acid-free, 250-year-life paper.

Printed in the United States of America

# "THE HIGHER CHRISTIAN LIFE"

## SOURCES FOR THE STUDY OF THE HOLINESS, PENTECOSTAL, AND KESWICK MOVEMENTS

*A forty-eight-volume facsimile series reprinting extremely rare documents for the study of nineteenth-century religious and social history, the rise of feminism, and the history of the Pentecostal and Charismatic movements*

Edited by
### Donald W. Dayton
*Northern Baptist Theological Seminary*

Advisory Editors
D. William Faupel, *Asbury Theological Seminary*
Cecil M. Robeck, Jr., *Fuller Theological Seminary*
Gerald T. Sheppard, *Union Theological Seminary*

*A GARLAND SERIES*

# PROCEEDINGS

## OF

# HOLINESS CONFERENCES

### HELD AT

## CINCINNATI, November 26th, 1877,

### AND AT

## NEW YORK, December 17th, 1877.

———— • ————

PUBLISHED BY
NATIONAL PUBLISHING ASSOCIATION
FOR THE
PROMOTION OF HOLINESS,
921 ARCH STREET.

J. S. INSKIP, Agent.

# HOLINESS CONFERENCE.

---

## CALL.

The following call was adopted by the National Association at Framingham, Mass. :

It is known to the friends of holiness that many persons
have suggested the propriety of a Holiness Conference, to be
held some time this coming autumn.

In order to give practical direction to these suggestions, a
committee was appointed at the National Camp-Meeting held
at Framingham, Mass., Aug. 15th, to prepare and issue a call
for such Conference.

In making this call, we remember with devout thanksgiving
to God, that such conventions have been held, both in this
country and in Europe, with many indications of the Divine
favor. We earnestly exhort all who are in sympathy with the
present efforts to spread Scriptural holiness over the earth, to
pray for the Conference, and, if possible, attend it.

It has seemed to many that such a Conference would give
opportunity for the presentation of the teachings of Scripture
upon this subject in such a manner as to correct certain er-
roneous views in regard to the doctrine and experience of
Christian perfection, and greatly promote the truth as it is in
Jesus. We invite the prayers and hearty co-operation of all
those who love our Lord Jesus Christ.

It is understood that all who respond to this call accept the
statement that entire sanctification is an instantaneous work

3

wrought in us by faith subsequent to regeneration, and attested by the Holy Ghost.

Rev. C. A. Van Anda, *Chairman.*

The following action also sets aside the first-named difficulty.

*Action of the Indiana State Holiness Camp-Meeting Association:*

On motion, Cincinnati was recommended as a suitable place for holding the National Holiness Conference.

On motion of Brother Jones, it was resolved to leave the preparation of programme for the " National Conference " to the "National Association for the Promotion of Holiness."

Warsaw, Ind., Sept. 19th, 1877.

Similar action, we are informed, was taken at the Ohio State Holiness Association and the Ohio Alliance.

This action, and a number of private communications, from different sections of the country, have induced us to announce the programme. First of all, we suggest that there be two conventions, or conferences, one at Wesley Chapel, Cincinnati, Ohio, commencing Tuesday, Nov. 26 ; the other at Willett St. M. E. Church, New York, to commence Tuesday, Dec. 17. This arrangement will accommodate the friends in both sections, and will secure a much larger attendance.

––––––

The National Holiness Conference, in pursuance of a call widely circulated through press and pulpit, met at Wesley Chapel, Cincinnati, O., at 7.30 o'clock, P. M. By arrangement of those who had the meeting in charge, Bro. John S. nskip led the evening devotional meeting, reading a part of John xv., and offering prayer ; the 290th hymn was sung,

followed by testimony, prayers, and praises, during which
" Heaven came down our souls to greet."

A committee of five, consisting of Bros. Larkin, Brooks
Lowe, De Pauw and Ricker, was appointed to nominate officers.

Adjourned with benediction, by Bro. Gillette, of Ind.

*First Day—Morning.*

A consecration and experience meeting was held from 9 to
10:30 o'clock, led by Bro. Inskip.   At 10.30 o'clock, the committee on nominations reported the following list of officers :

*President*—Rev. John S. Inskip.

*Vice Presidents* { Rev. John P. Brooks,
Hon. Thos. O. Lowe,
Hon. W. C. De Pauw.

*Secretaries* { W. T. Perkins,
Rev. Sylvester Weeks.

The President on taking the chair, read a portion of Acts
ii., and prayer was offered by Bro. John P. Brooks.

A committee of three, namely, Bros. Doty, Watson, and
De Pauw, was appointed to nominate a committee of five, to
prepare an address to the Churches, from the Conference.

The order of exercises, as determined by the programme,
was taken up, and a paper read by Bro. Wm. McDonald on

## ERRORS RESPECTING THE DOCTRINE OF HOLINESS.

### REV. W. MCDONALD.

Errors are *misapprehensions* or *perversions* of truth.   They
are theoretical or practical heterodoxy.   They may be harmless,

and they may be exceedingly disastrous. Their character must be judged of by their *effects*.

The doctrine of entire sanctification *has* always, and *will* always find earnest opponents, so long as "the friendship of the world is enmity to God." But that this opposition should come from those who accept the inspiration of the divine Word, which unqualifiedly declares, that "the blood of Jesus Christ cleanseth from all sin," is very remarkable.

It is not our purpose to deal with those who openly deny the possibility of heart purity in this life. But we shall consider the *errors* of such as profess to hold the doctrine, and yet so interpret it as to practically vitiate the truth.

We own it is not always pleasant to antagonize those you love and esteem as fellow-laborers in the kingdom and patience of Jesus. But this duty is forced upon every conscientious friend of holiness. He should earnestly contend for the faith, especially if he regards that faith vital—affecting the salvation of men.

In considering some of the more prominent errors respecting this subject, we notice :

1. *That which asserts that entire sanctification is co-etanious with regeneration,* or sanctification by the *wholesale.*

It is claimed by one class, that heart purity is complete at conversion ; it is insisted by another, that it is not complete until death. We pronounce both these extreme views equally false.

We shall here examine briefly the dogma which asserts that all sin or depravity is removed from the soul at conversion.

This doctrine is not more than 150 years old. We search the records of the Church in vain for a simple trace of it, earlier than that period.

Our object will be simply to ascertain the real *import* and *historic importance* of this dogma.

It had its origin, as most know, with Count Zinzendorf,

the founder and first bishop of the Moravian Church. He descended from a noble family of Austria; was born in Dresden, Saxony, May 26, 1700, three years the senior of Wesley. He was consecrated Bishop of the Moravian Congregation in Berlin, under the sanction of the King of Prussia. The *Count* spent nearly two years in America, returning in 1743. He died at Hernhut, May 9, 1760.

For a time Wesley was strongly allied to Zinzendorf and the Moravians, if, indeed, he were not one of them. He visited them at Hernhut, conversed freely with them, especially with Zinzendorf; and mainly on account of their views on the subject of entire sanctification, finally withdrew from him and them.

But what were Zinzendorf's real views on this subject? So far as we are informed, they are given by Wesley in these words: "We are sanctified wholly the moment we are justified, and are neither more or less holy to the day of our death; entire sanctification and entire justification being in one and the same instant."

In response to a question propounded by Wesley, in regard to the state of a believer, Zinzendorf says: "The moment he is justified he is wholly sanctified."

Mr. Wesley further represents Zinzendorf as saying: "All true believers are not only saved from the *dominion* of sin, but from the *being* of *inward* as well as *outward* sin, so that it no longer remains in them."

How far these views of Count Zinzendorf, which were resisted by Wesley all through his life, accord with modern writers on this subject, who sometimes affect to deny that they are Zinzendorfians, I leave you to judge, after a little. Dr. Crane, whose views in our judgment, are purely Zinzendorfian, says:

"Every one who is born of God becomes that very hour *a new creature, a new man, holy, free from sin, cleansed, sancti-*

*fied, saved."* He argues through many pages, that there is no *sin*, no *depravity* in him who is born of God.

This does not differ from Zinzendorf, who asserts, "that a man cannot have justifying faith, till he has, in a proper sense, a *new*, a *clean heart*," and that "all true believers are not only saved from the *dominion* of sin, but from the *being* of sin," "from the moment they are justified."

Dr. Crane, to avoid the imputation of being a Zinzendorfian, (for it requires no little degree of courage for one who wishes to be known and honored as a Methodist preacher, to come out and squarely antagonize a doctrine which Wesley very properly regarded as the great "*depositum of Methodism*,") insists that it was *imputed holiness* which Wesley opposed, and not the idea that depravity did not remain in him who is born of God, or justified.

He says: "It must be remembered that the holiness which he," (Zinzendorf) "described is *imputed*, not personal."

Dr. Whedon, in his attempted defense of Dr. Crane, repeats the same idea, giving the impression that Wesley only opposed Zinzendorf's notion of *imputed holiness*. But nothing can be more foreign to the real facts in the case, as the history plainly shows.

The fact seems hid, whether purposely or not we cannot say, from those who are not supposed to take the pains to examine for themselves, that Zinzendorf held the *two views ;* (1). "That we are sanctified wholly the moment we are justified ;" and (2). "That a believer is never sanctified or holy in himself, but in Christ only."

Wesley pronounced both these views contrary to the word of God and the experience of His children. But Wesley does not jumble these two ideas together as Drs. Crane and Whedon have done. Wesley opposes, generally, the first dogma, but seldom refers to the second. Referring to the second dogma, in a long conversation with Zinzendorf, Wesley insists that it is a strife about words. He says: "We contend, I think, about words." Again, "The dispute is altogether about words." But when Zinzendorf says: "A babe in Christ is as pure in heart as a father in Christ. There is no difference," this was not a strife about words. This was a thing to be opposed—refuted.

The *Quarterly Review*, which is set for the defense of the faith once delivered to the Methodists, in its July issue (1877) contains a defense of the Zinzendorf heresy. Of the *new birth* it says: "Every believer whose sins are truly forgiven, and who is begotten of God, is pure in heart, free from sin, and sanctified. And this sanctification is contemporaneous with the new creation."

This dogma Mr. Wesley directly antagonized in his sermon on "Sin in Believers." In that sermon, he urged: 1. That it was a *new doctrine*, and consequently, *false.* " It was never heard of," he says, " for seventeen hundred years; never till it was discovered by Count Zinzendorf. I do not remember to have seen the least intimation of it, either in any ancient or modern writer; unless, perhaps, in some of the wild, ranting, Antinomians."

2. He opposed it, as in his judgment, "A mischiveous doctrine," and "attended with the most fatal consequences."

He further says: "In 1739, while my brother and I were absent, certain men crept in among them, (his people) unawares, greatly troubling and subverting their souls; telling them they were in delusion; that they had deceived themselves, and had no true faith at all. 'For,' said they, 'none has any justifying faith who ever has any doubt or fear, which you *know you have;* or who has not a *clean heart*, which you *know you have not.'* "

In direct opposition to this, Mr. Wesley declares, that " a man may have justifying faith before he has, in the full sense, a *new*, a *clean*, heart."

He found at one time that many of his people, under the influence of this false doctrine, were giving up their hope in Christ. They were conscious of remaining depravity, and if this could not "remain in one that is justified," then they were not justified. Hence he says: "All, this week I endeavored also by private conversation to 'comfort the feeble-minded,' and to bring back 'the lame' which had been 'turned out of the way,' if haply it might be healed." (Vol. 3, p. 168). This must always be the effect of this doctrine.

3. *Wesley opposed the doctrine as unscriptural.*

Mr. Wesley says: "There are in every person, even after he is justified, two contrary principles, nature and grace, termed by St. Paul, the *flesh* and the *spirit*. Hence, although babes in Christ are sanctified, it is only in part. In a degree, according to the measure of their faith, they are spiritual; yet in a degree they are carnal."

And is it not marvelous that Dr. Whedon should interpret these words as meaning simply a *capacity* or liability for future sinning? He says: "*Liability* to *sinning* would be what Mr. Wesley would, as we understand, mean by the figure, '*Sin in Believers.*'"

No wonder Dr. Crane says: "If this be the doctrine of the sermon, I fully accept it." Well he may; but it is not the doctrine of the sermon.

With all due deference to the able and venerable editor of the *Quarterly*, we pronounce this interpretation of Wesley's language as great a perversion of its meaning as could well be made.

When Mr. Wesley speaks of "*infection of nature*," "*lust of the flesh*," "*corruption of nature*," "*sin remaining*," "*inward sin*," "*the seed of all sin*," "*sinful tempers, passions, or affections*," "*pride*," "*self-will*," "*love of the world*," "*lust*," "*anger*," "*peevishness*," "*carnal mind*," etc., does he mean, as Dr. Whedon affirms, only "*a liability to sin?*"

"*Liability*," means "*exposedness*." Men, whether *holy* or *unholy*, are *liable* to sin. But such *liability* differs widely from that "*lust*," "*pride*" "*anger*," "*corruption of nature*," of which Mr. Wesley speaks.

Dr. Crane attempts to prove that the sermon on "*Sin in Believers*" was written to "refute the notion that there is no sin in *any* that are justified." He argues that Wesley did not mean to say that sin did remain in *all* who are born of God, but only in *some*.

The very opening questions of the sermon refute this notion. Wesley inquires: "Is there then sin in *him* that is born of God?" "Does sin remain in *one* that believes in Him?" "Is there any sin in *them* that are born of God, or are *they* wholly delivered from it?" Whom does he mean by "*him*," "*them*" and "*they*," without any restriction? Common sense answers, *any one, all, every one*.

As though to directly antagonize Dr. Crane, Mr. Wesley further says: "I do not inquire whether a justified person may *relapse* either into inward or outward sin; but simply this: Is a justified or regenerate man freed from *all* sin as soon as he is justified? Is there then no sin in his heart? nor ever after, unless he falls from grace?"

To this question Dr. Crane and the *Quarterly* answer in the *affirmative*. John Wesley, in his sermon on "Sin in Believers," answers in the *negative*.

How such a dogma should ever have taken possession of any intelligent mind, with the Bible in hand, and experience in the heart, is a marvel.

It had its birth in the Antinomianism of Zinzendorf. If I accepted the dogma of *imputed holiness*, as he did, I could not accept of any other view of the subject. For as my holiness is not in *myself*, but in *Christ*, there could, of necessity, be nothing but *perfect* purity, if any purity at all, as there can be no *partial purity* in Christ. If we are complete or perfect in Him, in the sense of *imputed* and not *imparted* holiness, it must be a work done once for all.

Through this dark door of Antinomian heresy came this imp of night, which Wesley says is "attended with the most fatal consequences."

We have dwelt thus long on this error that we might ascertain its *origin* and *import*, knowing that these would stamp it as a bastard usurper.

We antagonize it because Wesley antagonized it. We discard it because it is alike opposed to reason, experience, and the Word of God.

2. *A second error, we denominate Salvation by Instalments.* Not a *completed* sanctification, but saved up to our light. No goal reached, only *approximated.* It is described thus: "He who walks most in the light of God will continually discover hitherto unseen evils in his heart." "Sin is progressively developed from the depths of unconsciousness into the light of God, where it can be dealt with by confession, pardon and cleansing."

It is admitted, to be sure, that "there is a definite crisis in many true Christian experiences, in which we present our bodies a living sacrifice, when Christ is formed in us; when in a deeper sense, to 'live is Christ.'" But then it is claimed that this should not be "held up as a '*higher* Christian life,' above the standard of *all* or *any believers*, but as THE *Christian* life, every other being a *lower* Christian life. We should not ask, 'Have I the higher Christian life?' but 'have I THE *Christian life?*'"

We will point out the fallacy of this dogma in a few particulars, without attempting an extended discussion of the doctrine.

1. It is a clear and emphatic denial of the higher life experience, which those who hold it are professedly seeking to promote.

If this experience is "not to be held up as a higher Christian life, above the standard of any believer," but "simply as

the *Christian life,*" in what respect does it differ from regeneration? That is *Christian life.*

It denies, as plainly as language can, anything like a definite experience subsequent to conversion, known and advocated as the "higher life." It is not enough for them to
speak of " *crisis* " in " Christian experience ; " for that does
not differ from any manifestation of God to the heart of
ordinary believers, when "new forms of depravity or sin
are developed from the depths of unconsciousness into the
light of God," and are " dealt with by confession, pardon
and cleansing." Any such manifestation may be called a
" crisis," in which we "present our bodies a living sacrifice."

The dogma reduces the higher life experience to simple
" growth in grace ; " nothing more.

2. *According to this doctrine we are never able to determine
when we are saved.* In fact, there is no evidence that we are
ever saved in this world.

If, as light increases, sin, or depravity is more and more
developed from the depths of unconsciousness into the light
of God, to be dealt with by "confession, pardon and cleansing," who can determine when the end of sin, or depravity,
is to come ?

As we may never come to the end of this increasing light,
so we may never come to the end of these new developments
of depravity. And as we cannot know that all depravity is
removed, unless we know that we have come to the end of all
light, which I presume can never be known, how are we to
know that the new light which falls upon us as our eyes open
in eternity, may not reveal new forms of depravity to confront
us on the threshold of our eternal home ? And even after
we have passed the eternal gates, how do we know that the
new and clearer light of that world may not discover hitherto unseen evils which will need to be dealt with by "con-

fession, pardon and cleansing?" Under such circumstances this would be a wonderful salvation.

3. We object to this doctrine further, because it teaches that our salvation is measured by our perceptions of our state, and not by God's revealed promise.

According to this doctrine, we are not saved, as we have been taught to believe, "according to the power that worketh in us," but according to the keenness of our vision—not to the "uttermost," but only so far as we can *see*.

When we pray to be "cleansed from all unrighteousness," reason teaches us that it is not a salvation limited by our knowledge, but by God's promises. If I am not able to see the depths of my depravity, *"He is able* who hath promised."

4. We object to this doctrine finally as unscriptural.

God nowhere reveals the fact that our salvation is measured by our light.

When Paul prays for the Ephesians, he does not pray God to save them up to their light, but "according to the riches of His glory." He desired that they might be able to *comprehend* with all saints, not more and more the "sin which is progressively developed from the depths of unconsciousness into the light of God," &c., but "what is the breadth, and length, and depth and height, and be filled with all the fullness of God." Then, to make the matter doubly sure, it is declared, that God "is able to do exceeding abundantly, *above* all that we *ask* or *think*," not according to our light, but "according to the power that worketh in us."

What, then, is the import of those Scriptures which assert that we are saved from "all sin," from "all unrighteousness," from "all filthiness of flesh and spirit," and "sanctified wholly?"

The promise includes all; and we ask "according to the promise." If *we* cannot see the bottom, God can, for no forms of depravity lie beyond His gaze.

5. Such an experience as we here controvert may very properly be said to be, not "the higher life." It is merely regeneration, with a life-long conflict with depravity. It gives up the doctrine of full salvation, and goes over, soul and body, to the old dogma of no complete deliverance from the *being* of inward sin while we remain in the body.

I am sure that whatever may be said of the doctrine, it is in direct conflict with the Word of God, and that is sufficient to stamp it as an error to be put away.

III. *A third error is one which asserts that entire sanctification is sin under control, and not sin exterminated.*

It is proper to say that persons holding this view are not very clear in their distinctions. Take as an illustration Dr. Whedon's definition of sanctification. "Sanctification is such a measure of power *over sin* as holds us with more or less continuity in the same perfect fulness of Divine approbation as rested upon us when justification first pronounced us, through Christ, perfectly innocent of sin."

The Doctor's metaphysics translated would read something like this: "Sanctification is the continuance, with more or less interruption, of our full justification."

If a believer succeeds in maintaining his first justification, with more or less, interruption, he is sanctified.

There are many and grave objections to this theory.

1. *It is anti-Wesleyan.*

This might not be an objection to it with many, but with loyal Methodists it is a serious objection.

It confounds entire sanctification with the Wesleyan idea of justification.

In one of Wesley's early conferences, (1744) the following question was introduced and discussed, viz.:

"What are the immediate fruits of justifying faith?" "*Justifying,*" mind you.

*Ans.* Peace, joy, love, *power over all outward sin, and*

*power to keep down inward sin."* This is *repression,* but it belongs to *justification* only.

"The justified," says Mr. Wesley, *"has power both over outward and inward sin, from the moment he is justified."* "The immediate and constant fruit of the faith by which we are born of God," says Mr. Wesley, "fruit which cannot be separated from it for an hour, is power over sin;—power over outward sin of every kind; and power over *inward* sin." This is *repression.* So it would seem that the *Quarterly,* in its description of entire sanctification, has only reached Mr. Wesley's idea of justification.

2. *The dogma is unscriptural.*

It is affirmed on good authority that there are no scriptural terms applied to *inbred sin,* which signify *repression.* "The Greek language," says Dr. Steele, "richly abounds in words signifying *repression;* a half-score or more occur in the New Testament, yet none of them are used of *inbred sin;*" but such *verbs* as signify to *cleanse,* to *purge,* to *purify,"* &c.

"Repressive power is nowhere applied to the blood of Christ, but *purging, cleansing, washing, making pure,"* &c.

3. The fallacy of such a dogma is seen in that it makes the uninterrupted continuance of *one* thing, *another* thing. In other words, it makes the uninterruptedcontinuance of justification, with now and then a fall, entire sanctification.

It denies the doctrine of sin as a *state,* and resolves it all into acts. It does not accept the doctrine of *depravity* at all. Justification respects *acts* not *states.* The doctrine of universal Christendom is, that there is depravity lying back of our acts from which they spring.

4. *We notice, finally, a fourth error, which we denominate* the *wolf in sheep's clothing theory.* This is generally known as *imputed* holiness, or holiness by *proxy.*

Outside of those who hold with the Methodists on this subject, this is a wide-spread error. The manner of stating it is *specious*. It has the voice of Jacob, but the hands of Esau.

It claims that "sanctification is not the purifying of the flesh, but the outgrowth and development of the new man." It is the Christ-life in us, but not the old man destroyed. We are perfect *in* Christ, but not in ourselves.

If by not being perfect *in* ourselves, it means that we cannot be perfect *of* ourselves, then the statement is correct. But there is a marked difference between being perfect, or holy *in* ourselves, and being holy *of* ourselves. It is an *imparted* holiness—a holiness *from* Christ, not *in* Him in the sense of not being imputed to us.

And yet, over all this land, and others as well, it is being taught that our *defilement* is not *removed*, only *covered*. Perfect love is not our love made perfect to Christ, but His love made perfect to us.

There are many and unanswerable objections to this dogma.

1. There would be no reason in the Apostle urging believers to "go on unto perfection," if the doctrine be true that believers are perfect because Christ is perfect for them.

2. The Scriptures speak of some who are perfected, and of others who are not yet "made perfect in love;" but if believers are perfect in Christ, they would all, of necessity, be equally perfect.

3. Believers are exhorted to "be perfect in every good work. Are we to understand that to be "perfect in good works" is the same as being perfect in the person of Christ? It cannot be that they are one and the same.

4. This doctrine teaches holiness by proxy. We are full of sin, but Christ is pure. God does not see us, He only sees Christ. The unspotted garment of Christ's holiness covers up all our defilement, and we appear like a whited sepulchre,

fair without, but within, full of corruption and dead men's bones.

We *obey* by proxy. So long as Christ's obedience is accepted by the Father, our acts go for nothing—they are not seen by God, nor is any account taken of them. So long as Christ does not sin, we are safe, if we simply believe that He is such a Saviour *for* us, and *to* us.

Mr. Fletcher very properly says: "If we obey by proxy, we may sin as much as we please; for it is plain that if the obedience of another be accepted in lieu of our own, while we continue to indulge in a slight degree of sin, it may be thus accepted if we indulge in a little more, and so on, until we have reached the depth of transgression."

There is no avoiding this conclusion. The Scriptures declare with great clearness that we may be "cleansed from all filthiness of flesh and spirit." The "old man may be crucified," the "body of sin destroyed." But pray, how does this accord with the idea that the "flesh is still present in all its original sinfulness, and will remain unholy to the end?"

We have, in a brief and imperfect manner, presented a few of the more prominent errors which greatly embarrass the subject of holiness. As holiness becomes more and more a subject of interest, errors respecting it become more and more bold, requiring careful and thorough exposure. If we would have this subject triumph it must be divorced from all such errors as we have named, as they are fatal to its life.

We urge upon all the duty of guarding this doctrine against errors both theoretical and practical; first, by keeping the experience in the heart and life, and the theory in the intellect, so that both may go hand in hand, until the "*Mighty to save*" shall fully reign in all hearts.

On motion of H. O. Sheldon, the Conference requested the paper for publication.

2 o'clock was fixed as the hour for the afternoon session, the hour from 2 to 3 o'clock being spent in discussion or devotion ; the printed programme to be strictly adhered to as regards the hours and subjects announced.

A communication from Brother S. Baker, giving the reasons for his absence, was read by the Secretary, and referred to a committee of two, who were instructed to send a fraternal response to Brother Baker. Brothers McDonald and Watson were appointed the above committee.

*To the Conference of the Friends of Holiness, to be held in Wesley Chapel, Cincinnati, Nov. 27, 1877.*

Dearly Beloved Brethren : Grace, mercy and peace be multiplied unto you. It would give me great pleasure to be with you, to enjoy your Christian fellowship, to hear your sanctified discussions of sacred truth, and to receive your godly counsels and prayers, but our Heavenly Father sees proper, for wise reasons, to will otherwise. In view of this, I have been requested to furnish to the Conference a written communication upon any subject I might deem important. I deem all of those subjects important which mark the distinctive features of the " Holiness Movement ;" and the questions to come before the Conference, so far as they are named in the programme, are matters upon which I entertain very decided convictions, and which I regard as having a very important and vital connection with the redemptive work committed to the Church. I do not, however, feel competent to prepare a paper, upon any of these themes, that would edify the Conference, and will not consume its time by any attempt of the kind. The only thing I now feel it would be proper to do, as most honoring to the Lord under the circumstances, is to state, as briefly as I can, the remarkable rest of soul, and victory over suffering, which a perfect trust in a perfect Saviour has secured to me.

By a case of obstinate Rheumatism, I have been almost entirely disabled for nearly all of the three past years. During that time I have been confined to bed for five consecutive months, have been confined to a wheeled chair for a still greater length of time, and for the last eighteen months have been able with great difficulty to walk a little by the aid of crutches. The prospect before me in the .natural order of things, is permanent and hopeless decrepitude; and with all this, though constitutionally a very pushing and active man in every department of life, I am perfectly contented, rejoicing evermore and glorying in my infirmities. When I have been unable to attend Church service, which has been the case for many months at a time, the loss of that privilege has been compensated by such realizations of the "exceeding abundantly above all we ask or think," that I felt no need of the communion of saints so necessary in a state of health. Though my sufferings have been very great at times, I have enjoyed almost a continuous and uninterrupted feast—a kind of "National Camp Meeting" in my soul all the time.

For this faith, this knowledge of the way into the holy of holies, and for this wonderful secret of living happy in every state and condition of life, I am largely indebted, under God, to the writings and teachings of very dear brethren of your Conference who may now be listening to the reading of this humble ackowledgment. I need not state, therefore, that I am very greatly attached to them, and all other workers on this line; and that all I have and am, are fully, and forever, consecrated to the work of spreading scriptural holiness over these lands.

Though I have but fairly entered the primary classes, and caught a general view of the wonderful workings of the more advanced departments, I find the school of Christ a marvelous institution. A glimpse into the department of suffering has thrown new light upon all those afflictive dispensations so generally deplored by mankind. Poverty, disease, persecution, and every other cause of suffering, I now see, are golden opportunities for the development of Christian character, and ought to be pressed into service by the believer, with more eagerness than artists seize whatever will aid them in perfecting their art. It now seems a most fatal mistake to prostitute these providences to the very common purposes of arousing envy, murmuring, and resentment, instead of using them for personal religious culture and discipline. They are also endowments or qualifications for doing good to others, like money, health, and social influence, only of a different class, and for their proper use we shall be held to as strict account as for any other form of talents. They are not only to be used, as from their very nature they may be, in the development of the loveliest graces in ourselves, but for wooing others also to a life of devotion by an exhibition of the Christliness of patient and joyful suffering. My afflictions which seem to some of my friends unmitigated evils to be deeply deplored, I have found to be a divine reordination to the high commission, of teaching others the happy art of rejoicing amidst suffering, and of bearing to them some of the sweetest secrets of the divine bosom.

I, therefore, feel in no haste to escape from my present promotion, though some other would have suited my preferences better ; and while I ardently solicit an interest in the prayers of my very dear brethren of the Conference, it is that I may more efficiently glorify our adorable Lord, in sickness or health, in life or death, or in whatever way His grace and wisdom may choose.

I earnestly hope, and shall most devoutly pray, that your Conferences in Cincinnati and New York may be seasons of great grace, and by the blessing of God may give to the cause of Christian holiness in our country new and mighty impulses that shall soon be felt in every station, and upon every circuit, in the wide field of American Methodism. That these impulses may the sooner be felt, and that we who have been denied the gracious privileges of your meetings, may be benefited as well as gratified, I trust the Conference will provide, before its adjournment, to furnish the reading public interested in the spread of the Redeemer's kingdom, a summary of its proceedings.

With the deepest solicitude for the final triumph of Christianity, and in the profoundest sympathy with all engaged in the work of extending the light and joyful experience of Christian purity among the. struggling captives of an enfeebled faith, I am, in the freedom of perfect love,

Your peaceful and happy brother,

S. BAKER.

On motion of Brother Doty all papers coming before the Conference were referred to the editors of the National Holiness Association. Brother Doty was, by vote, requested to preach this evening, at 7.30 o'clock, in place of Brother Baker, who is providentially detained at home.

Adjourned with the Doxology. Benediction by John P. Brooks.

---

*First Day—Afternoon.*

The Conference was opened by singing

"All hail the power of Jesus' name!"

followed by prayer by Bro. Alonzo Campbell, of the Rock River Conference.

The minutes of the previous meetings were read, and approved.

The President, having announced that further discussion of the subject of the paper read in the morning was in order, remarks were made by several brethren.

The Committee appointed to nominate five brethren to prepare an address to the Churches, named the following, which nomination was approved :

J. P. BROOKS, WILLIAM McDONALD, J. C. WEIDMAN, E. T. WELLS, G. D. WATSON.

Bro. Watson, of Evansville, Ind., addressed the Conference on the topic assigned him :

## ENTIRE SANTIFICATION SUBSEQUENT TO REGENERATION.

### REV. G. D. WATSON.

There is no dispute as to the fact that sanctification is a work initiated and begun in every regenerated soul. When a soul is born from above, there is planted within it the Divine life, but it is not the fulness of life, or the " life more abundant."

There is planted in every new-born soul the germs of every Divine grace ; but those graces have not the complete mastery of the heart, and are not entire.

We do not mean by entire sanctification a mature sanctification. An apple may be an entire apple and yet not a mature apple. When Joshua crossed the Jordan, he was *entirely* in the promised land, but was not maturely there, for the land was not yet divided and occupied. So entire sanctification is having the entire being of the body, soul, and spirit; entirely devoted to the entire will of God, with an entire trust that Jesus entirely cleanses from moral evil, and an entire confession to this entire work. This is what I understand to be entire sanctification.

Now in attempting to show that this work in its entirety is not coetaneous with the new birth, I ask attention to the following proofs :

*1st. All the Biblical analogies of the work of grace,* show that entire sanctification, (or its synonym) is subsequent to conversion. In the epistle to the Hebrews, in the fourth chapter, we have a concise analogy between the Hebrew pilgrimage and Christian experience, where Egypt answers to the bondage of sin, Sinai to adoption, and Canaan to the rest of faith, which is a synonym of entire sanctification. In the 9th and 10th chapters of Hebrews, another analogy is drawn between the Tabernacle and Christian experience, where the first veil, which is the holy place, answers to conversion, and the second veil, or most holy place, answers to the perfecting of holiness, which is a synonym of entire sanctification.

Another analogy of grace is that of heirship—the law of heritage. In many places in Scripture, the word "inheritance" is used as a synonym of the fullness of the Gospel blessing. (See Acts 26 : 18. Eph. 1 : 13–14. Col. 1 : 12). Now we know that we must first be born before we can claim and possess our inherited property.

The inducting in kingly or priestly office forms another analogy, and "anointing is a synonym of entire sanctification." (Ex. 40 : 15. Acts 10 : 38. 2 Cor. 1 : 21. 1 John 2 : 27). But the Prince could not be anointed King without having previously a royal birth, either Divine or human ; and one must be born of a Priest before he could have a priestly anointing.

In all these analogies we see that the synonyms which answer to entire sanctification are by necessity subsequent to that which answers to the new-birth.

*2d. The removal of guilt from a moral criminal, and his*

*reconciliation to God, is an essential pre-requisite to the imparta-
tion of Holiness to the soul.* Pardon removes all guilt, entire
sanctification removes the latent impurity of the carnal mind,
and the outer crust of actual guiltiness must be taken away to
prepare the way for a work of cleansing upon the latent nature
of the soul. God can entirely sanctify an infant and take it
to Himself at His will, for the infant has committed no actual
sin to block the pathway of the sanctifying Spirit. But
where actual sin has been committed it blockades the channel
of the Spirit, and must be removed to prepare the way for
God's deeper work. We could muster an army of Scripture
passages to prove this point. We will select a few. "Nevertheless, there are good things found in thee, in that *thou hast
prepared thine heart to seek God.*" 2 Chron. 19: 3.

"So Jotham became mighty, *because he prepared his ways*
before his God."

"O Lord, keep this in the thoughts of the heart of Thy
people, and *prepare their heart unto Thee.*"

"And Samuel spake saying : If ye do return unto the Lord
with all your hearts, and *prepare your hearts* unto the
Lord."

"If iniquity be in thine hand, put it far away. If thou
*prepare thine heart*, thou shalt lift up thy face without spot."
Job 11: 13–15.

"His going forth is *prepared* as the morning." Hos. 6: 3.

The previous words show that this going forth is in personal experience, and teaches us that a soul must first be
restored to daylight before it is prepared for the full orbed
manifestation of Jesus. In Rom. 9: 23, we see that God
makes known the riches of His glory on the vessels of mercy
which had been previously prepared for this glory, the word
glory here, being as in many other places, a synonym for the
baptism of the Holy Ghost ; so that no heart can receive the
baptism of the Holy Spirit without a preparation. In 2 Tim.

2

2 : 21 we are are told what that preparation is. "If any man purge himself from these, he shall be a vessel unto honor, sanctified, and meet for the Master's use, prepared unto every good work."

It is evident from reason and Scripture, that entire sanctification cannot be wrought, until the soul has been prepared for it by previous removal of guilt and by reconciliation.

In Acts 2 : 38 Peter asserts plainly that remission of sin was a prerequisite for the gift of the Holy Ghost.

3d. When man has gone astray from God by actual transgression of His law, *his moral nature and religious understanding are not able to endure at one step the complete and compound change from guilt to entire purity and the fulness of the Spirit.* Entire sanctification involves a great deal more than most Christians ever dream of, and if it were wrought at the moment of conversion, then the *mind* would have to apprehend such a number of moral facts, the *heart* would have to feel such a number of penetrations, the *conscience* would have to bear such a double stream of spiritual light, the *faith* would have to grasp such a stretch of Divine promise and power, the *self abnegation* would have to make such a sudden leap into a sense of nothingness, and above all, the *emotions* would have to stand the shock of such a double surge of ecstacy, that it would require an extraordinary miracle on the *intellectual* and *physical* frame to make them equal to the experience ! We find ample proof on this point in the "true sayings of God."

"And it came to pass, when Pharaoh had let the people go, that God led them not through the way of the land of the Philistines, although that was near ; for God said, Lest peradventure the people repent when they see war, and they return to Egypt." Ex. 13 : 17.

How plainly this agrees with advanced experience, and teaches us, that in the Canaan of entire sanctification our faith must endure a stress which at the moment of conversion would probably drive us back to the world.

And Jesus answered them saying: "All men cannot receive this saying, save they to whom it is given. He that is able to receive it, let him receive it." Mat. 19 : 11–12.

When the mother of James and John petitioned great things, Jesus gave them to know that their unrenewed nature could not yet bear the burden of such things. ' Ye shall indeed drink of my cup and be baptized with my baptism, but ye are not yet able."—Matt. 20 : 22. Nor were they able to enter such an utter crucifixion to self till after their regeneration.

"And He spake the word unto them as they were able to hear it."—Mark 4 : 33. "Jesus answered him, whither I go thou canst not follow me now, but thou shalt follow me afterwards. Lord, why cannot I follow Thee now? Jesus answered, wilt thou lay down thy life for my sake?"—John 13 : 36.

Entire sanctification implies a hearty willingness to promptly lay down our lives for Jesus, at any time. Is the penitent praying for pardon ready for such utter self-abnegation? Jesus positively affirms that we *cannot* yet enter such a consecration. Again, Jesus affirms that the world, that is unregenerated men, cannot receive the baptism of the Holy Spirit !—John 14 : 17. We are taught in this passage, that we have no moral capacity for entire sanctification until after our regeneration. Paul says to certain converts in Corinth, " I have fed you with milk, not with meat ; for hitherto ye were not able to bear it, neither yet now are ye able, for ye are yet carnal." 1 Cor. 2 : 30.

*4th. No one ever wants or prays for entire purity and sanctification, till after he has gone through regeneration.*

God does not supply spiritual gifts where there is no felt want, no apprehension, and no prayer for the gift. No one feels his need of holiness, no one apprehends the deep necessity of holiness, no one has been known to pray for holiness, except those who had been pardoned. In the very nature of the case, entire purity does not come within the scope of a penitent sinner's vision ; so that we ·must be reconciled to God before we will begin to pray for entire sanctification.

*5th. The Holy Spirit cannot teach us of our inward need of holiness until after we have been born of the Spirit.*

In the work of entire sanctification the heart must be taught of God, and there must be moral revelations made to the heart, which the Spirit can teach only to those who are in the kingdom of God. We must be first kingdom born in order to receive kingdom tuition. The Holy Ghost must first raise our spiritual nature from death to life, before He can disclose to us the profoundest needs of our nature. This agrees with what the Spirit says, " Awake thou that sleepest, and arise from the dead, and Christ shall give thee light."— Eph. 5 : 14. Here, the in-streaming of spiritual light begins at conversion, but it is that very spiritual light which is to teach us of the latent evil of our being, and of the necessity of inward purity and of the fullness of love. The teaching of the Holy Spirit in the heart consists of two departments, viz : the human and the Divine. In a state of regeneration, the Spirit teaches us of our needs, deficiencies, evil pronings and utter helplessness. In a state of entire sanctification, the Spirit not only continues teaching us our nothingness, but He teaches us of the riches and fullness of God. He teaches us of the clear personality, power, sweetness, and interior life of the Adorable Jesus. When we are born again, we enter the kingdom of God; when we are entirely sanctified, the kingdom fully enters into us. When we are regenerated, we learn our true spiritual wants, when we are entirely sanctified we learn of God's inexhaustible supply.

Jesus told Nicodemus that he had to be converted before he

could begin to learn these inner spiritual lessons ; saying, in substance, " if I have told you of your earthly needs, and you do not understand (because not converted), how can you understand if I tell you of the heavenly fullness?"

*6th.* No one is ever commanded to be holy ; none are urged to entire sanctification, except those who are already recognized to be God's people or God's children. The Bible commands sinners to repent, commands penitents to believe, and commands all believers to be holy, to go on *to perfection,* (not toward perfection).. The abiding gift of the Holy Spirit is promised only to God's children, so that adoption must precede the baptism of the Spirit. All the intercessory prayers in the Bible for entire sanctification, whether offered by Christ or the Apostles, were for those who had previously been converted.

*7th.* The Discipline of the Methodist Episcopal Church *teaches most explicitly that entire sanctification is subsequent to regeneration.* In the Discipline of 1876, on page 3 it is said, " In 1737 they saw, likewise, *that men are justified before they are sanctified;* but still holiness was their object. God then thrust them out to raise up a holy people." This statement is the official utterance of the doctrine of the M. E. Church, that sanctification is a spiritual blessing to be obtained after justification. On page 97, we find in the questions to the traveling Preachers, after the question, " Have you faith in Christ?" which of course must mean converting faith, for it would make the Church blush with shame to think she were obtaining unconverted Preachers ; after the query comes the question, " Do you expect to be made perfect in love in this life?" Here the Church teaches that perfect love is a blessing to be sought and obtained in this life, subsequent to conversion. Again, on page 252 in our Ritual for the baptism of infants, after recognizing the infant as being included in the spiritual covenant of God, a member of the kingdom of heaven, and therefore in a justified condition our Ritual prays that God would *wash* and *sanctify* this child.

All these, and many other passages that might be quoted, prove that it is the official statement of Methodist faith that entire sanctification is a blessing to be obtained in this life subsequent to regeneration.

*8th.* To this line of evidence may be added, in conclusion, that of *experience.* In all the generations of religious people, whether in the Bible or out of it, there has not yet been found one solitary *clear testimony* as to the coetaneousness of regeneration and entire sanctification, even those who affect to teach the theory that these two blessings are coetaneous, do not support the theory with their own clear personal testimony. Among those who teach that entire sanctification is a blessing obtainable after (we would not say how long after) conversion, *there are many of us who know it with the certainty of cloudless noon !*

---

Additional remarks were made by several brethren.

After the doxology the benediction was pronounced by Bro. H. O. Shelden.

*Evening.*

After an hour's devotion, the Conference heard a sermon from Bro. Doty from Gal. ii. 20, and after an exhortation by Bro. Inskip, altar exercises were held, and while we communed before the mercy-seat the unction of the Holy Ghost came upon us and we were enabled to rejoice with joy unspeakable.

Benediction by Sylvester Weeks.

*Second Day—Morning.*

The Conference convened at 9 o'clock, and was opened by

the members quoting passages of Scripture expressing thanksgiving, or the occasions of thanksgiving.

Testimony and experience followed, till the hour fixed for the printed programme arrived.

At 10.30 o'clock, with Bro. Inskip in the chair, after the reading of the minutes, it was, on motion, resolved that a committee of seven be appointed to take into consideration the subject of combining in some way, in harmonious action, the various organizations interested in the holiness movement. The selection of that committee was assigned to a committee of three : Bros. McDonald, Brooks and Rowland.

On motion, Brother G. D. Watson was requested to supply the lack of service of Brother Creighton, who is officially detained, by preaching this evening at 7.30 o'clock.

The Conference resolved, by common consent, to hold at this hour, a thanksgiving service.

After a thanksgiving anthem by the choir, the lxvi. Ps. was read and the meeting opened for expressions of thanksgiving, by praise, or prayer, or experience, or testimony.

An hour was spent in this joyous service, at the conclusion of which the Conference adjourned to the hour of 3 p. m.

The Doxology was sung, and the benediction was pronounced by Brother Gillette.

---

### Second Day.—Afternoon.

Conference reassembled, the president in the chair. After singing and prayer, led by Brother C. W. Rowland, Brother Inskip made a few remarks touching the nature and object of the present Conference.

Rev. E. T. Wells, of Dayton, O., then read to the Conference his paper upon the assigned topic.

# DOES THE HOLY SPIRIT WITNESS TO THE EXPE-
RIENCE OF ENTIRE SANCTIFICATION?

### REV. E. T. WELLS.

" *Thy Testimonies are very sure: holiness becometh thine house, O Lord, forever.*"—PSA. xciii. 5.

The testimony of the Holy Spirit to a truth is given directly and indirectly. Indirectly through the Word and directly to the heart, by mysterious but sure communication.

This twofold testimony of the Holy Spirit to the doctrine and experience of entire sanctification is ours. That the Spirit witnesses to this truth in the Word, will not be denied. It will not be necessary to quote any of the many scriptural texts which teach entire sanctification as a possible experience in this life.

We have to do in the question before us, with the direct witness of the Spirit to the heart.

The first direct witness of the Spirit to this experience is found in the *conviction* which comes to a soul of its possibility, its obligation, and its blessedness ; creating in us a strong desire for it as a personal possession, and impelling us to seek for it.

The Spirit reveals to us our sinful condition ; causes us to cry, "unclean, unclean," and to pray with perseverance and mighty concentration for that which we now believe possible by a clean heart. All of which is the testimony of the Spirit in us to its truth. As one has eloquently said, " The impulse in the bird to fly south, is *evidence* that there is a south to fly to." The impulse of the soul to holiness is the witness of the Spirit in that soul that there is holiness for it. In obedience to this impulse it spreads its wings for unwearied, persevering flight, knowing that it shall find the genial clime of full salvation.

This impulse lifts it up to things above: "It bears on eagle's wings," and by the inward conviction "it sees all the land below."

> " Rivers of milk and honey rise,
>     And all the fruits of paradise
>         In endless plenty grow."
> " A land of corn and wine and oil,
>     Favored with God's peculiar smile,
>         With every blessing blest,
>     There dwells the Lord our righteousness,
>     And keeps His own in perfect peace
>         And everlasting rest."

The Spirit witnesses directly to our hearts in His convicting and awakening power.

Again, the Spirit witnesses directly in our hearts to the work wrought in us. The direct witness of the Spirit with our spirits that what the Word declares is possible, and what we have been led to desire and seek after, is ours in the experience which we have received.

There is a conscious change in the soul from pursuit to possession. From inquiry to understanding. From going to arriving. From seeking to finding. From investigation to knowledge. He now knows this thing which was freely given to him of God to know, and he knows it by the Spirit which is given unto him. He is not now a seeker in the same sense in which he was before. He has the undoubted testimony within to his arrival at the destination. The Spirit who has been his guide witnesses to him that this is what he was after. When he interrogates his blessed leader to be assured that he is right in reckoning himself saved from sin, the Spirit floods his soul with light, and so clear is the evidence that he would be untrue to think or declare anything to the contrary.

This interior evidence is not the result of reason, not the

conclusion of a logical process. He was not arguing when he received it.

It is not an inference from observation of the fruits of the Spirit in us. Before we have passed through any tests and antecedent to all activity, in a quiet, trustful attitude of mind we know that this work has been done by direct witness of the Spirit.

It is not an imagination or fancy, for the mind was not acting in that direction. There was great want in the soul, not exuberance of fancy. It was in no condition to evolve such an experience or conception, not active, but waiting. In this condition it clearly recognized a power without itself and not of itself coming in and cleansing the place. Instead of imagining this we stand still and see the salvation of God. Joseph Cook says—"I assert that it is a fixed natural law, that when you yield utterly to God, He streams into you, gives you a new sense of His presence and imparts a strength unknown before." What proofs have we to this affirmation of *the direct witness* of the Spirit to the experience of entire sanctification? We answer reason, the Word of God, and Christian experience.

1. It is not unreasonable to suppose such a witness. We are capable of receiving it, and God is able to give it. This is declared explicitly in that scripture which says, "The Spirit itself beareth witness with our spirits that we are the children of God." This settles the fact of the possibility of such direct witness to our personal salvation. You may say, however, that this is a witness to a degree only of salvation, to the beginning, to regeneration. We admit that, but does it not establish the divine order and make it reasonable to conclude that God will witness to the grace, whatever it may be, into which we come? Will God witness to justification and give the soul no witness to that which is beyond justification? Will that which was begun so brightly and with such

assurance grow dim and vague and indefinite as we proceed?
"The path of the just is as a shining light that shineth *more*
and *more* unto the perfect day." Will justification which is
sanctification begun, be witnessed to, and cleansing, which is
sanctification completed, be without the witness? Are we
sure of a witness to partial sanctification and not sure of a
witness to entire sanctification? The whole is greater than
any of its parts, but if there be no witness of the Spirit to
entire sanctification then the part is in this particular greater
than the whole, and has a quality not found in the whole
which is the sum of all the parts. This is an impossibility.

"The inward witness, the inward," cried Samuel Wesley,
"is the proof, the strongest proof of Christianity." We may
add holiness, holiness, is the crowning glory of Christianity,
that which in a supreme sense becometh God's house, but if
there be no inward witness to its experience, then our greatest
glory is left without our strongest proof. We are irresistibly
driven to the conclusion that the evidence of the higher must
equal that of the lower experience. That the sunlight of the
witness which falls on the foundation gilds also with its
brightness the top-stone of God's building within us. The
witness of our childhood in Christ is not greater than that of
our manhood in Him.

Then again, God's plan of salvation is not a changing,
shifting plan in its conditions and evidences. Men are not
justified in one way and sanctified in another way.

There are certain great factors that are always found at
every stage of the plan, and we believe the witness of the
Spirit to be one of those constant factors. For instance it is
always by faith, and always through Christ in the plan
wherever we are. "The just shall live by faith." "The
righteousness of God is revealed from faith to faith." I
should as soon expect to find a place in the onward progress
of religious experience where faith or Christ were no longer

conditions as to find a place where the witness of the Spirit was withheld. We have the plan of salvation up to the point of justification well analyzed. All its steps are marked, all the features are brought out. We have conviction, confession, renunciation, faith as conditions precedent, then we have justification, regeneration, adoption and the witness of the Spirit as the concomitant blessings. But when we turn to sanctification as a distinct work we seem to think it has no conditions precedent nor blessings concomitant. We see the state but the roads to it are not very well defined. We think perhaps we change the plan here and leave the track, getting out of the express train of God's rapid transit for the soul by faith in His mighty power and go the rest of the way on foot without a guide. Ask your converted friends and you will find, perhaps from their views, that there are half a dozen ways of getting sanctified. One will say, "Well, I think we are first converted and then grow in grace until we grow into the experience of sanctification." Another will say, "It is by attention to duty, going about doing good like the blessed Master, a plan of works and self-endeavor." Another will say, "It is by some geometrical progression in which one day will be better than the last, and by accumulating goodness, getting better and better, we shall finally attain the second experience." Thus do we who began in Christ expect to be made perfect some other way. The fact is, and true theology finds that the conditions precedent to sanctification are similar to those of justification. There is primarily deep conviction of the inbeing of sin, of the remains of the carnal mind, there is confession of this condition, there is renunciation so far as a disease can be renounced, and there is faith in Jesus and in Him alone for sanctifying power. There follows as a result, cleansing, rest, perfect love, Baptism of the Holy Ghost, witness of the Spirit all concomitants of sanctification. I should as soon expect this great distinct work of grace without conviction or faith, as without the witness of the Spirit. It is a prominent and constant factor of God's unchanging plan.

We take it that the doctrine of the witness of the Spirit which meets us at the very door of the Christian life, is not to be simply the evidence of our having entered but also the witness to our onward progress. What we found true at the first stage of our experience will be true at every stage. The declaration direct of the first witness is proclamation of the law of the witness of the Spirit, that is over the entire Christian pathway. How clearly this is shown by Bunyan in Pilgrim's Progress, which all will admit to be a most faithful representation of Christian experience. We see him in company with one Interpreter who explains many things to him ; we see him before the cross where his burden fell ; we see the three shining ones as they stand before him. One says, "Thy sins are forgiven," another strips him of his rags and clothes him with a change of raiment, the third gives him a roll which he was to look upon as he ran. This roll we are afterwards told was his assurance, or witness of the Spirit that gave him comfort ; farther on he comes to the Palace Beautiful from whence he is shown or witnessed to the Delectable Mountains, which he is told will further add to his comfort, because they were nearer the desired haven than the place where at present he was. He asked them the name of the land ; they said it was Immanuel's land, " and it is as common," said they, "as this hill is, to and for all pilgrims." When at last he arrived *at the mountains*, and beheld the gardens and orchards, the vineyards and fountains of water ; where also they drank, and washed themselves, and did freely eat of the vineyards, they were not satisfied with all these evidences that were fruits of the place, but drew nigh to the shepherds to inquire, " Whose delectable mountains are these and whose be the sheep that feed upon them ? " They wanted a witness, an assurance, it came in the answer of the shepherds, "These mountains are Immanuel's land, and they are within sight of His city. And the sheep also are His and He laid down His life for them." Here was corroborative testimony to the direction received at the Palace Beautiful, and with all the evidences around them was the witness of the Spirit to the land they were in. What means all this guidance and instruction along Christian's pathway in this beautiful allegory, but that the Spirit witnesses to every place or experience into which we come.

We must have this witness to save us from uncertainty and suspense and give us sweet rest and satisfaction. It is needed as much if not more than the first witness—to save us from deception, that we may not stop short of the fullness, neither be unable to recognize it with certainty when we receive it. I was once possessed with a desire to see a certain grove of giant trees in the mountains of California. I had the witness by word of their existence, and the inner conviction of its truth. Yet when ready to penetrate the mountains and find the kings of the forest, a guide was necessary to show the way and tell us when we had found them. For we must remember we are seeking for trees among trees. A special variety scattered among other trees, and never isolated from other species. They are disseminated among pines, spruces and cedars. As we ascend and approach the neighborhood where they are found, we pass many wonderful and tremendous trees not of this variety which we seek. So great were many of these that at last we should have been unable with certainty to have decided when we had found the locality. Without the guide, our witness, we would perhaps have stopped short of our object, concluding we had found when we had not, or we might have gone on and on and on, passing the very objects of our search, and yet not being sure but there were others still greater beyond. Without our guide we should have pitched our tent too soon, or wandering in restless uncertainty, have returned with no certain knowledge whether we had seen or not.

Likewise the soul with the testimony of the word as to the trees of righteousness of the Lord's planting, and the inward desire to see them, commences to climb and ascend the hill of the Lord. Seeking for that which is never isolated from other experiences. Seeking religion in religion, trees among trees, where there is life and verdure, a forest of wonderful growths and experiences all around us. A great many teachings and experiences not of this variety. There is that Zinzendorfian tree which many mistake for this. There is the tree of restraining grace or repression, which is a good-sized tree, judging from the numbers and ability of many who camp around it. The tree of imputed holiness which deceives many, for it looks as large as any in the forest. The tree of installments, that adds a circle every time it gets a deeper look into itself. There is the tree of gradualism, a kind of Century Plant. No one ever lives long enough to see it in blossom. It may bloom but the living witnesses to the fact are not to be found. There are so very many excellent trees like Apollos—who was mighty in the Scripture, fervent in spirit, yet—"knowing only the baptism of John." We should be confused without a witness. As the soul goes on in its upward course, the foliage is richer, the trunks are larger, we may come to a halt just this side. We may have blessings so large that our souls would say this is the place, or we might seek on and never be able certainly to say we had found. Never be sure but there might be something more complete beyond. We would have a large memory of blessings, but no certain knowledge whether we had had *the blessing*.

God gives us a guide to lead us into all truth. He tells us when we come upon the delectable mountains. He tells us where to pitch our tent and spread our table and content ourselves. Where the water is cooler and the growths are not to be surpassed. He tells us when we stand in sight of the great truths, we open our eyes and our souls to them, they grow upon us the longer we stay, we abide and take in and absorb and assimilate and develop, knowing that we have reached the place which God had revealed to us in His Word. We sought, we found. We know that we have found by the testimony of the Spirit who was our guide.

God witnesses as directly to the soul upon reaching this Canaan of perfect love, as He did to His people in the wilderness when they had arrived at the earthly Canaan. He declared to them through Joshua, that this was the promised possession. He described its boundaries, "From the wilderness and Lebanon, to the great river on the north and the great sea toward the going down of the sun, shall be your coast."

He did not lead His people on an uncertain expedition, toward an Eldorado of promise which they could never certainly identify. He did not leave them to infer from the general terms of the promise that any certain locality must be the one sought. He declared to them the place, henceforth no more wanderings, but rest and permanancy and certainty is their's. This is well understood to be typical of the second work of grace in the heart and in the spiritual leading of the soul out of Egypt and into Canaan. God will witness to that soul its arrival at the land of promise, and cessation from wandering will be its portion.

2. The next source of proof we shall notice of the witness of the Spirit to the experience of entire sanctification is the Word of God.

All the passages of Scripture which relate to the office work of the Holy Spirit. " He shall guide you into all truth. A guide must be a witness to the places into which he guides. The soul cannot know truth certainly unless it be attested by the Spirit. *"All truth,"* that must include sanctifying truth, as a guide, then He must witness to that truth in the experience, for a soul is not guided into a truth until it experiences it.

"Now, we have received not the spirit of the world, but the Spirit which is of God ; that we might know the things that are freely given to us of God." Sanctification is one of the things freely given to us of God, and it is the office of the Spirit to make us know that we have received it.

"Which things also we speak, not in the words which man's wisdom teacheth, but which the Holy Ghost teacheth ; comparing spiritual things with spiritual." Here is declaration that the Holy Ghost teaches the words or names of the things which God gives. Will not this same Spirit apply these names to the experience which He works in our hearts? And if there be a wonderful salvation within like a tonic to the Spirit, giving great might and power to the inner man, will not the Spirit tell him this is sanctification? He will speak the word in the soul which He speaks in the teaching of the Word.

"But the anointing which ye have received of Him, abideth in you, and ye need not that any man teach you ; but as the same anointing teacheth you of all things, and is truth, and is no lie, and even as it hath taught you, ye shall abide in Him." What can this refer to but the direct communication of the Spirit to the heart? The Spirit, teaching, witnessing, and so clearly as to satisfy without the corroboration of man. The anointing brings its own evidence, and the soul sanctified by the baptism of the Holy Ghost is clearly taught what it received.

This witness is proven in the Word because it makes the experience of entire sanctification and the baptism of the Holy Ghost concomitant. The one is a fruit of the other. We might as well ask, does the Holy Ghost witness to the baptism of the Holy Ghost ? Can He interpret His own operation ? " Now He that hath wrought us for the self-same thing is God, who also hath given unto us the earnest of the Spirit.''.

In the Scriptural history the experience of purity came with the baptism of the Holy Ghost. The first baptism in the wilderness, after which they received Christ and were given power to become the sons of God, was a baptism of repentance unto remission. " To as many as received Him to them, gave He power to become the sons of God."—John, 1. To those who were born of the Spirit and were followers of Christ, there remained an additional baptism and work. At the very baptism of John, which was pardon and acceptance, there came a cry of another baptism in addition : " He shall baptize you with the Holy Ghost." To these, John baptized disciples and candidates for the baptism of the Holy Ghost, there came a new word, not of remission, but of cleansing, not " now are ye forgiven," but " now are ye clean." There came for them a new prayer, not " Father forgive them," but "sanctify them through Thy truth." There was before these disciples yet as a new experience, cleansing, sanctification and baptism of the Holy Ghost. On Pentecost day these were all made clear to their experiences. With that mighty baptism came the sanctifying, purifying power, and with it the witness of the Spirit to the work wrought. This is shown by the testimony of Peter, afterward when recounting the reception of the same baptism by Cornelius and his friends. Peter says, " And God, which knoweth the hearts, bare them witness, giving them the Holy Ghost, even as He did unto us ; and put no difference between us and them, purifying their hearts by faith." What could be plainer than this, that the baptism of the Holy Ghost was a purifying work and that in that baptism God bore them witness to the sanctified state of their hearts, " knowing their hearts bare them witness," direct Scripture to the fact that the Holy Ghost witnessed to their purification. Peter said "God gave them like gift as unto us." Hence Pentecost was purity, and they had the witness of the Spirit to that effect.

In the Epistles we find this same coupling of the work of sanctification with the gift of the Holy Ghost and the corresponding evidence thereto. Paul says to the Corinthians, " Now he which stablisheth us with you in Christ, and hath anointed us, is God, who hath also sealed us, and given the earnest of the Spirit in our hearts."

What is this stablishing and sealing coupled with the anointing, which was the baptism of the Holy Ghost, but the experience of sanctification? What is the earnest of the Spirit, which may be rendered pledge of the Spirit or evidence of the Spirit, but the inward witness of the Spirit? Clarke says in substance on this passage, " From this unction and sealing we have a clear testimony in our souls to our salvation."

Again, " In whom also, after that ye believed ye were sealed with that Holy Spirit of promise, which is the earnest of our inheritance, until the redemption of the purchased possession unto the praise of His glory." Here is something which occurred after conversion. Something experienced by those who had heard the Word preached and had trusted it. "In whom also," that is, in addition "after they had believed " they were sealed with that Holy Spirit of promise, which is the earnest of our inheritance. " Clarke says of this passage, " That this Spirit of truth makes the impression of His own actual purity and truth in the souls of them who believe and thus they bear the seal of God Almighty." Also, he says, " This earnest of the Spirit is the witness of the Spirit."

That the sealing of the Spirit which is the earnest of our inheritance, is the witness of the Spirit to sanctification will appear from two passages of Scripture which make the inheritance the portion of the sanctified. Paul said to the elders of Ephesus, "And now, brethren, I commend you to God and the Word of His grace which is able to build you up, and to give you an inheritance among all them which are sanctified." Also Paul declared before Agrippa, that God had sent him to the Gentiles, "that they may receive forgiveness of sins, and inheritance among them which are sanctified by faith that is in me." The inheritance depends upon previous sanctification. The sealing of the Spirit "after that they believed" was the sanctifying work, and the earnest of the inheritance, was the witness of the Spirit to that sanctified condition which makes meet for the inheritance of the saints in light.

What can better illustrate this witness of the Spirit than the figure of sealing? Our standard definition of the witness of the Spirit is, "An inward impression on the soul whereby the Spirit of God immediately and directly witnesses to my spirit that I am a child of God." What can more beautifully illustrate this inward impression than the sealing? What a clear impression stamped upon the wax or paper by the seal. How sacred the seal. The King's seal must not be broken. If we are sealed we have the inward impression of God's image within. The direct and immediate witness that we are His. "Purified unto Himself, a peculiar people."

3. We have as proof of this doctrine of the witness of the Spirit to the experience of entire sanctification, the teaching and testimony of many who have enjoyed this blessed experience.

Mr. Wesley clearly taught it as will appear from the following: To the question, "But how do you know that you are sanctified, saved from your inbred corruption?" Mr. Wesley replies, "I can know it no otherwise than I know that I am justified." "Hereby know we that we are of God," in either sense, "by the Spirit that He hath given us." "We know it by the witness and by the fruit of the Spirit."

"None, therefore, ought to believe that the work is done till there is added the testimony of the Spirit witnessing his entire sanctification as clearly as his justification." "As when we were justified the Spirit bore witness with our spirit that our sins were forgiven, so when we were sanctified He bore witness that they were taken away."

Dr. Adam Clarke says : "Wherever this Spirit comes, it bears a testimony to itself. It shows that it is the divine Spirit by its own light ; and he who receives it is perfectly satisfied of this. It brings a light, a power, and conviction more full, more clear, and more convincing to the understanding and judgment, than they ever had or ever can have, of any circumstance or fact brought before the intellect.

The man knows that it is the Divine Spirit, and he knows and feels that it bears testimony to the state of grace in which he stands." "This Spirit in the soul of a believer is not only manifest by its effects, but it bears its own witness to its own indwelling. So that a man not only knows that he has the Spirit from the fruits of the Spirit, but he knows that he has it from its own direct witness."

Charles Wesley has taught us to sing

> " I want the witness Lord,
> That all I do is right,—
> According to thy will and word,—
> Well pleasing in Thy sight."

Dr. Geo. Peck says in his work on " Christian Perfection," " I shall now proceed to present what I conceive may be considered satisfactory evidence of a state of entire sanctification.

1. The witness of the Spirit—the testimony of God's Spirit that the soul is entirely sanctified. Among other things he then says : " If a sensible evidence of adoption may be expected, then the same kind of evidence may be expected

with increased lustre, to accompany the different stages of our progress in holiness. If God vouchsafe to the merely justified an evidence of gracious acceptance, would He be likely to withhold from those, whose hearts are entirely consecrated to Him, an evidence that the offering is accepted? Indeed the doctrines of the evidence of adoption, and of entire sanctification in this life, being proved, it seems a matter of course that the inward testimony of the Spirit to the truth of the latter, whenever it takes place, would be afforded."

Dr. Steele, speaking of this experience says : " The soul, amid the intensity of this spiritual illumination, enjoys an assurance of salvation which could not be increased were that fact written by Gabriel in letters of fire across the arches of the sky."

" No amount of testimony, human or angelic, can increase the certitude of the soul lit up by the presence of the Comforter. We do not need lanterns to see the sun rise. He brings his own self revealing light." " I no longer doubt Wesley's doctrine of the direct witness of the Spirit as distinct from the testimony of my spirit discerning the fruits of the Spirit and inferring His presence and work." " If sin consists in a state, as some with truth assert, when they describe original sin, I infer that I am not in such a state, from the absence of sinful energies flowing therefrom, and *more especially from the* indwelling of the Holy Spirit." So much for the teaching of those who knew whereof they affirmed. What says experience—the most authoritative proof next to God's Word that we can have? Joseph Cook says : " It should be asserted by science in the *name of experiment that man* may become a partaker of the divine nature." The truth of this doctrine rests on experience. Let Lady Maxwell speak ; she says : " The Lord has taught me that it is by faith, and not joy that I must live. This has diffused a heaven of sweetness through my soul, and brought with it the powerful witness of purity." Carvosso quotes this passage, and remarks upon it: " I have recorded these remarks, because they so perfectly agree with my own views and experience." "Two more competent witnesses in a case of this kind could scarcely be desired," says Dr. Peck.

In a volume called " Riches of Grace," where sixty-two experiences are recorded, let me give a few who have spoken on this point.

Rev. J. I. Pettee says: " The blessing was mine—I felt I possessed it. The witnessing Spirit supplanted my convictions, and I experienced a deep assurance that my prayer was answered, and the blessing bestowed. Felt conscious that I had given all for Christ, *and felt the witness of the Spirit*, like an impression on my soul, that He had become 'all in all to me.' "

Another witness says: " It was not joy but peace. So sure I felt of my acceptance, such a *witness* that my soul was cleansed, so sweet was the peace of God that it was beyond the power of language to express my feelings."

Another. " I received the *witness of the Spirit* by believing the work already done."

Another. " The Holy Spirit seemed increasingly to witness with my Spirit that the work wrought in me was of a purifying nature."

Dr. Upham, a man of keen intellect, who was not early trained to believe in the witness of the Spirit says, after coming into this experience, "I have continually, what seems to me, to be the WITNESS OF THE Holy Spirit; that is to say, I have a firm and abiding conviction that I am wholly the Lord's; which does not seem to be introduced into the mind by reasoning, nor by any methods whatever of forced and self-made reflection, which I can ascribe only to the Spirit of God. It is a sort of interior voice, which speaks silently but effectively to the soul and bids me be of good cheer."

Another who received this blessing and its mysterious witness which is like the wind " which bloweth where it listeth " —seemed to be fanned by a Heavenly Breeze, and put into verse his experience as follows. With this we conclude, hoping our readers may ever be conscious of this blissful gale wafting them heavenward.

### A HEAVENLY BREEZE.

It comes! it comes! I know not why!
  The wings of love divine surround me,
And God is stooping from on high
  To shed the air of heaven around me.

It brings a calm, a Christ-like peace,
  Mid inward music sweetly flowing ;
It whispers, " Free, and sovereign grace
  This *heavenly breeze* is now bestowing."

I feel it, ay, most mild and sweet,
  In charming movements gliding o'er me ;
It circles round my heart's retreat,
  And fans away the mists before me.

It is not fancy that deludes,
  'Tis no impulsive flight of feeling,
'Tis no illusion that intrudes,
  But 'tis the Holy Spirit's sealing.

Come Holy Spirit, waft along
  A constant gale that shall surround me,
And roll, while seraphs tune their song,
  The atmosphere of heaven around me !

Still let me have this lamb-like frame,
  And bask amid Thy beams' bright shining,
And feel Thy love's encircling flame,
  My heart with Thine in union twining.

So shall I dwell in heaven below,
  And drink Thy full salvation pouring :
On blissful gales to God I'll go,
  And fall before His throne adoring.

The Conference joined heartily in singing the Doxology, "Praise God from whom all blessings flow."

Remarks upon the topic were made by Rev. Bro. Ricker, of Iowa; Rev. Dr. Watson, of Indiana; Rev. Wm. McDonald, and Rev. J. P. Brooks, of Illinois, and others.

Mr. Carr, of I., appointed at morning session to nominate a committee of seven, reported the following nominations, who were appointed:

| | |
|---|---|
| W. T. PERKINS, | G. D. WATSON, |
| W. C. DE PAUW, | J. P. BROOKS, |
| WM. McDONALD, | THOS. K. DOTY, |

C. W. ROWLAND.

Adjourned with benediction by Bro. Ricker.

———

*Second Day—Evening.*

At 7.30 P. M. a sermon was preached by Bro. G. D. Watson, of Indiana, from the text 1 John iv. 18. Altar exercises were held, a number presenting themselves as seekers of full salvation, some of whom entered into the rest of faith.

Benediction by Bro. Ricker.

———

*Third Day—Morning.*

A prayer and testimony meeting was held from 9 to 10.30 o'clock, closing with a service of consecration, during which the Lord revealed the right arm of His grace and power. Bro. Ricker was requested to preach at 7.30 P. M. in place of Bro. Scheutz.

The order of the programme was taken up and a paper read by Bro. Sylvester Weeks, on the subject:

3

# HOW MAY ENTIRE SANCTIFICATION BE RETAINED?

REV. S. WEEKS.

Nature and grace, originating in the same heart and thought, both clearly demonstrate that God never created anything, animate or inanimate, soulless or spiritual, without making abundant provision for every legitimate demand of His creature. Does He create birds? He feeds them; does He make the lilies? He clothes them; does He form the human spirit, permitting it to take its being with a sinful nature, yet in its sin with aspirations and longings, boundless, restless and insatiable, and then leave it, the noblest of His creatures, without provisions for its need? nay verily He that openeth His hands and satisfieth every living thing is more willing to give His Spirit to them that ask Him than earthly parents are to give good gifts unto their children—more ready to respond to a conscious want intelligently expressed, than to simply meet the instinct or necessity of the soulless thing. Assuming as a fact substantiated by inexorable logic, certified by conscious experience, and, better than both these, for logic may have its flaws, and experience its defects, God's word, the Holy Bible plainly, by type, and promise, and provision, and command, and example, presents entire sanctification as a doctrine to be believed, and an experience to be attained by man, in this present evil world.

It has been clearly shown, from reason and from revelation, that holiness is a possible experience in this life; that it is subsequent to regeneration; that it is instantaneous, being an act of God; and that the Holy Spirit gives His witness to the work. Now the practical question is, does God provide all this, merely to lift the soul for a brief season to a Pisgah summit, permitting it to taste and see the length and breadth, and height and depth of the Redeemer's love and the blessed Spirit's power, and then send it down to the sin-soiled experience of the past, to remember, with sad heart and weary longing, the *moment* of rest from sin, and to look forward to the valley of the shadow of death as the avenue to the only place in the universe where it may *abide* in His love?

Poor soul of man, if this be thy heritage, ascend the mount, realize the full baptism, shine a moment in the radiance of that glory, and then, down like a captive to thy work-day clothing and thy never-completed struggle against sin, and as thou bearest the burden, from which a death-purgatory alone can free thee, sing, if thou hast heart to sing:

> " Oh ! those happy, happy *moments*,
> How *glad* they were !
> Oh ! these weary, weary *years*,
> How *sad* they are."

The Bible teaches the unity of the human race; that is, not merely that God made of one blood all men, but, that the race in its entirety, from Adam to his latest posterity, is one; hence we find the great All-Father dealing with this unit, which we call humanity, as the parent deals with the individual of the race; as we recognize in the individual the four periods of infancy, childhood, youth and manhood, and as we seek to educate and develop through and with these four periods by object lessons, for the infant; commands, for the child; promises, for the youth; and intuitions, for manhood; so God develops the race through its infancy by types; through its childhood by the Law, through its youth by principles, and into its manhood, where spiritual perceptions guide, and, at the same time, advance it. To illustrate: going back to the beginning, we find that man, having sinned, sought to prepare himself by works of his own to meet his God; but he found the fig-leaf covering of his own devising insufficient, and the offended Father coming in "the cool of the day" and calling for His child as in former days, brought out the confession, "I was afraid, because I was naked;" but when "the Lord God made coats of skins and clothed them," then the fear was gone and the consciousness of want of preparation taken away: thus the first pair by object lessons are taught that *blood-shedding* of the *sinless* would alone provide a *covering* in which they might meet their God.

Then again in the sacrifices made by Cain and Abel the whole stress of the narrative lies on "the gifts"—the objects; these men were *brothers*, sons of the same parents, their education, surroundings, and the example before them precisely the same; they brought their offerings to the same God —the one is accepted, the other is not—where lies the difference? The book of Hebrews declares explicitly: "By faith Abel offered unto God a more excellent sacrifice than Cain, by which he obtained witness that he was righteous, God testifying of his gifts; and by it he being dead, yet speaketh" (Heb. "is yet spoken of"—i. e., the salvation abides to this day). Cain's offering was bloodless, a thank-offering, suitable to the sinless or the pardoned, but not proper for the guilty, or the unforgiven. The Lord said to Cain, "If thou doest well, shalt thou not be accepted? and if thou doest not well, sin lieth at the door (a sin-offering croucheth at thy door)."

The teaching of the whole is that God accepts the *offerer* for the sake of the *offering*. No man may be saved by works; nor can any man begin in the Spirit and be made perfect by the flesh.

God's development of salvation, running through types, commands, principles and intuitions; through the ceremonial law, the moral law, the sermon on the Mount, and the epistles, in which, always the last revealed, includes all that has preceded it; just as in nature, the acorn, the twig, the sturdy sapling, and, at last, the giant oak, are successive manifestations of one design in which each includes all that goes before it; indicates that each stage is retained till the time for fruition with the next beyond. In saving the soul we have

**P** ENITENCE.
**A** RDON.
**E** ACE.
**U** RITY.
**O** WER.
**A** RADISE.

There is no completed salvation without penitence, retained till pardon is secured; there can be no conscious salvation without peace, no restful salvation without purity, no useful salvation without power, no eternal salvation without paradise; and it must be perceived that each of these includes (that is, retains) all that goes before.

The Bible abounds in declarations of God's intentions toward His people, and it is notable that in the New Testament, there are no directions given to a soul on the retreat; all commands and all promises are based upon abounding grace, responding to states of the soul, attained and retained, till by their very retention the felt want calls out the apprehending faith, and the upward step is taken.

The ceremonial observances of the Jews all indicated purity, maintained as long as the conditions were met by which it was attained. The Jewish worshiper brought his offering, laid his hands upon its head, thereby showing that he transferred his guilt, or more probably that he expressed his oneness with the gift; the animal was slain, setting forth thus, the desert of the offerer, that he could be saved, only by putting a death between himself and God: the burning of the victim upon the brazen altar, the very word altar, in its etymology conveying the idea of slaughter, taught clearly that the presenting unto God of that which was slain for sin, secured pardon ; the laver with its washing of the feet that were to walk in the holy place, and of the hands which were to minister there, taught purity ; the shew-bread (the word of God), lighted-up by the seven golden candle-sticks (emblem of the Spirit), prepared the way to the altar of incense (the symbol of acceptable prayer) that stood before the veil. The High Priest bearing upon his shoulders (the emblem of strength) and upon his breast (the emblem of affection) the names of the twelve tribes of the people of Israel, went once a year into the immediate presence of the Shekinah, the visible representative of God. He being accepted, all who were represented in him, by their birth, or by their compliance with the conditions of worship, were accepted with him. This acceptance continued till the offering lost its efficacy, the offering being valid, by divine appointment, for one year. But let it be noted any one might make null and void the efficacy of the offering by his own act, incurring guilt and thus cutting himself off from the accepted nation.

" For the law having a shadow of good things to come, *and* not the very image of the things, can never with those sacrifices which they offered year by year continually, make the comers thereunto perfect.

For then would they not have ceased to be offered? because that the worshippers once purged should have had no more conscience of sins.

But in those *sacrifices there is* a remembrance again *made* of sins every year.

For *it is* not possible that the blood of bulls and of goats should take away sins.

Wherefore, when he cometh into the world, he saith, Sacrifices and offering thou wouldest not, but a body hast thou prepared me :

In burnt-offerings and *sacrifices* for sin thou hast had no pleasure.

Then said I, Lo, I come (in the volume of the book it is written of me) to do thy will, O God.

Above, when he said, Sacrifice and offering and burnt offerings and *offering* for sin thou wouldest not, neither hadst pleasure *therein;* which are offered by the law ;

Then said he, Lo, I come to do thy will, O God. He taketh away the first, that he may establish the second.

By the which will we are sanctified through the offering of the body of Jesus Christ once *for all.*

And every priest standeth daily ministering and offering oftentimes the same sacrifices, which can never take away sins :

But this man, after he had offered one sacrifice for sins, for ever sat down on the right hand of God ;

From henceforth expecting till his enemies be made his footstool.

For by one offering he hath perfected for ever them that are sanctified.''

That is if the offering is imperfect, the power of it is limited as to time, but if it be absolutely perfect (as in the offering of Jesus), then the efficacy is perpetual.

We repeat God looks not so much at the *offerer* as at the *offering*, while that retains its saving virtue, the offerer retains all that he secured through it, unless he, by his own act, rejects it.

The commands of the Bible at the same time set forth the fact that holiness may be retained, and answer the question, how may it be retained ?

The examples are numerous, e. g. in *Gal. v. I*, we are commanded to ''stand fast in the liberty wherewith Christ hath made us free, and be not entangled again with the yoke of bondage,''—from the context we learn that the freedom is obtained by casting out the son of the bond woman, being assured that *that* which ''is born after the flesh persecutes that which is born after the Spirit," and that to tolerate, or educate, or repress, is to have galling bondage, but to cast out and keeps out the evil-nature is to have freedom.

In Col. ii. 6 : " As ye have received Christ Jesus the Lord, so walk in him."

God does not command us to do that which we cannot do, hence we may walk in the Lord ; attain a standing in Him, and retain that state.

" Abide in me, and I in you.  As the branch cannot bear fruit of itself, except it abide in the vine : no more can ye, except ye abide in me.

I am the vine, *ye are* the branches : He that abideth in me, and I in him, the same bringeth forth much fruit : for without me ye can do nothing.

If a man abide not in me, he is cast forth as a branch, and is withered ; and men gather them and cast *them* into the fire, and they are burned.

If ye abide in me, and my words abide in you, ye shall ask what ye will, and it shall be done unto you.

Herein is my Father glorified, that ye bear much fruit ; so shall ye be my disciples.

As the Father hath loved me, so have I loved you : continue ye in my love.

If ye keep my commandments, ye shall abide in my love ; even as I have kept my Father's commandments, and abide in his love.

These things I have spoken unto you, that my joy might remain in you, and *that* your joy might be full."

The promises of God's word assure us that we may retain all to which we attain, God's power and truth being pledged thereto.

John x. 27–29 : " My sheep hear my voice, and I know them, and they follow me, and I give unto them eternal life (not duration, but quality) ; and they shall never perish, neither shall any pluck them out of my hand. My Father, which gave them me, is greater than all; and none is able to pluck them out of my Father's hand." While the Father will not cast them out, and no power can pluck them out of the Father's hand ; we may *take* our cause out of His hand, by our volition ; hence, unless we withdraw our suit, we remain in the Father's keeping, and retain that state of soul that placed us there.

In 1 John i. 7 we read, "If we walk (walking is an act requiring will-power to determine it, and exertion to execute it, it is a steady, uniform, progressive motion)—if we walk in the light, as he is in the light, we have fellowship one with another (like the radii of the circle approaching the centre, the more intimate our fellowship with God, the nearer we are to each other) ; and the blood of Jesus Christ his Son cleanseth us (keepeth us clean) from all sin."

Then, too, the spiritual intuitions pointed out in the Bible all establish the possibility of retaining sanctification by showing us the test.

John vii. 17 : "If any man wills to do his will, he shall know of the doctrine, whether it be of God ;" he that deliberately and persistently intends to do the will of our Father, shall be led into all requisite knowledge. John viii. 32 : "Ye shall know the truth, and the truth shall make you free "—not truth abstractly considered, but the truth as it is in Jesus ; the truth must be known, not apprehended by the mind ; that form of knowledge is very liable to error and uncertainty, but the knowledge we gain in conscious experience not merely sets free, but makes free. The proclamation of emancipation could free four millions from bondage, but did not and could not qualify those freed for their freedom. John xvi. 13 (in passing—another quotation from John, no wonder, Matthew gives the words of Christ, Mark gives the works, Luke gives the spirit, John gives the nature): " How be it, when he the Spirit of truth, is come, he will guide you into all truth—he will show you things to come.'' In Romans viii. 14 it is written : '' For as many as are led by the Spirit of God, they are the sons of God ;'' now the carnal mind cannot discern the leadings of God's Spirit, for they are spiritually discerned.

In I. Cor., ii., 9-10 we have the glad words : ''Eye hath not seen, nor ear heard, neither have entered into the heart of man, (*i. e.*, into the imagination of man), the things which God hath prepared for them that love him. But God hath revealed them unto us by his Spirit ; for the Spirit searcheth all things, yea, the deep things of God.''

So that by the Bible in types, and commands, and promises, and in its response to our profoundest spiritual call for guidance, meets us and shows that God has abundantly indicated His will that we may retain whereunto we have attained in spiritual things.

1. In order to retain entire sanctification we must avoid the neglect of the use of the powers and faculties which constitute us men.

If God gave us

JUDGMENT,
CONSCIENCE,
AFFECTIONS,
and WILL,

and these in their union make our personality complete, then, since God will judge us, as persons, not our surroundings, or inherited tendencies, or depravity, He expects and requires us to use these component facts of our complex being in determining the highest interests with which we have to deal, our soul's salvation.

It is for the judgment to investigate and decide upon the truth; the conscience to yield to it ; the affections to embrace it, and all these operations of mind, or conscience, or heart, to be performed under the direction and concurrence of the will.

We cannot retain holiness in its purest, highest acceptation while the judgment is in error ; the voice of conscience, telling us what to do and what things to leave undone, is disregarded ; while the affections are in the least estranged or while the will is crownless and scepterless.

II. To retain holiness there must be no willful nor needless exposure to moral contamination; if God's guidance takes us into the fiery furnace, He will see that no smell of fire lingers on our garments, if He leads us to a den of lions, He will demonstrate to adversaries, that no God can deliver as can the God of Daniel ; if He permits us, or takes us to Potiphar's house, He will see to it that in immaculate virtue we shall sit in Pharaoh's house.

III. We are to avoid a religion of mere *resolution* by which we undertake, by strength of will to keep ourselves ; equally unsatisfactory is the religion of repression, by which in the ceaseless vigilance of untiring activity we are to crush back sin in its first manifestation, and thus with hands fettered be debarred the privilege and pleasure of helping another.

IV. We are to avoid censoriousness—the Lord no more confines Himself to one mode of working in grace, than He does in nature; He may reveal Himself to others as He does not unto us ; and He may bind us around with restrictions which He does not impose upon others, and may place burdens upon us which others do not have to bear. Entire sanctification does not consist in meats, and drinks, and costumes, but in righteousness, and peace, and joy in the Holy Ghost.

V. We cannot retain entire sanctification, and, at the same time, withhold our full sympathy from any phase of true Christian experience, despising or lightly esteeming "the little ones" who believe in Jesus. Perfect love is accompanied by that humility that will take lessons any where.

VI. We cannot retain the blessing and wilfully neglect the means of grace ; "such are—the public worship of God ; the ministry of the word, either read or expounded; the Supper of the Lord; prayer; searching of the Scriptures," and that temperance which keeps the body under.

When one gets into that dreamy fanaticism which professes to rise superior to God's appointed means, we can no more live and grow than can the physical man live without the food appointed of God to nourish him, nor develop without the exercise demanded by the very constitution of his being.

Having noticed the negative side of the question, let us look at it in its positive aspect.

I. To retain entire sanctification there must be a continual, complete and joyful submission to the will of God.

II. Confession—doing this not to exalt self, but to magnify the grace of God, the power of Jesus' blood, and the cleansing efficacy of the ever-blessed Holy Spirit. It is vain for us to say that we will let our lives testify; we may have a correct outward life, a voice modulated to tones soft as the lute, and as musical, and a cheerful countenance, and all these may be but the expression of a happy, easy-going nature; or they may be the simulations of one with sinister motives, or they may be the fruit of holiness. How are those without to know our secret unless our mouths confess?

In Rom. x. 10 it is pointedly declared: "With the heart man believeth unto righteousness, and with the mouth confession is made unto salvation." The heart is the life-centre of our spiritual being, so that we believe, or rather trust, when the *judgment* gives its verdict for Jesus; the *conscience* gladly bows to Him; the affections with eager joy flow forth to his advances; and the *will*, the sovereign, puts itself and all beside into His keeping, to be, to do, to suffer, and every mountain of our redundancies is brought low, and every valley of our deficiencies is exalted, and the rightful King, Jesus, with all our powers and passions, voluntary and involuntary, and even our tastes, and appetites, and imaginations, following glad captives in His triumph, takes the realm, but the salvation is not complete till we proclaim Hlm King. One may be born a prince, be anointed and crowned, but he is not king till he is proclaimed and acknowledged.

The temple of Solomon may gleam in the morning sunlight in its beauty of marble and gold ; it may stand as having been erected for the God of Israel—the materials and the skill, and the men who furnished both may be and were all the Lord's—but there was no token of divine acceptance till Solomon, the mouth-piece of the nation, acknowledged it the Lord's, THEN the glory filled the house.

Without confession the pure gold soon becomes dim.

Your last confession, rendered your due unto the Lord up to that time, but what of the mercies and blessings since?

When you cease believing, or God ceases saving, then you may stop confessing, not till then.

If we confess Him, He will confess us. The blood-washed and white-robed in heaven, overcame "that old Serpent, called the Devil and Satan," and cast him down, "by the blood of the Lamb, and the word of their testimony."

III. We can only retain holiness by activity—2. *Pet., i.* 4-8.

"Whereby are given unto us exceeding great and precious promises ; that by these ye might be partakers of the divine nature, having escaped the corruption that is in the world through lust.

And besides this, giving all diligence, add to your faith, virtue ; and to virtue, knowledge ;

And to knowledge, temperance; and to temperance, patience ; and to patience, godliness ;

And to godliness, brotherly kindness ; and to brotherly kindness, charity.

For if these things be in you, and abound, they make *you that ye shall* neither *be* barren nor unfruitful in the knowledge of our Lord Jesus Christ.''

Neither *idle* nor unfruitful. Let the joy of the Lord be your strength.

IV. Our consciousness, and the godly estimate of our brethren must be one and the same as to our standing ; thus shall we avoid the appearance of evil, whether it be in the direction of spiritual pride, or in singularity in dress, or extravagances in statement of doctrine, or experience, or in our manifestations.

V. By suffering patiently.—*Phil.*, *i.* **29** *: ii.* 8.

"For unto you it is given in the behalf of Christ, not only to believe on him, but also to suffer for his sake ;

"And being found in fashion as a man, he humbled himself, and became obedient unto death, even the death of the cross."

VI. And finally we may retain sanctification by regarding it not as the end, but as means to an end, that end being the glory of God, then, whether it be care or pain, life or death, earth or heaven, God is glorified, and the soul is satisfied.

*Et teneo et teneor.*

Enoch lived three hundred and sixty-five years; three hundred of these years he walked with God. ("Can two walk together except they be agreed ?"—can God agree with an unsanctified man?) walked with God three hundred years, and one day walked home with God and never came back to earth. Peace as a *river* retains and receives.

The locks at the lakes. How may the ships retain that higher level? By staying there. How may entire sanctification be retained? By keeping it.

The essay of Bro. W. Jones of Toledo, which, in his necessary absence, was not read at the time assigned yesterday, was read by Bro. Thomas K. Doty, the subject being :

# IS ENTIRE SANCTIFICATION AN INSTANTANEOUS OR A GRADUAL WORK?

REV. W. JONES, M. D.

The embarrassments that environ this subject would all disappear if we would be more accurate in the use of terms. Our words, correctly defined, should be the true exponent of a specific mental conception.

The Bible speaks of a state of grace variously denominated "Holiness," "Purity," "Perfect Love," "Entire Sanctification." These terms are never used interchangeably with the word regeneration; hence we discover that *entire* sanctification is a part of our complete salvation not accomplished BY the act of regeneration.

The process of entire sanctification is that of cleansing—the condition of the sanctified soul is that of purity—the experience of entire sanctification is the consciousness of the individual that he has been cleansed from *all sin*, and that he is *now pure*, as a result of the process through which he has passed. Webster defines sanctification as the act of *God's grace* by which the affections of men are purified from sin and exalted to a supreme love to God. The word entire is a qualifying term—indicating the degree of purity attained, or the extent of sanctification experienced. According to the Lexicon, entire is a term signifying completeness,—in all its parts "full," "perfect," "comprising all requisites in itself," "without defect." According to this definition, *entire* sanctification is a state of unalloyed purity of heart, a condition of completed renovation of the moral nature.

This work of complete restoration of moral purity to the soul is either an instantaneous work wrought by the power of God, or it is a gradual process.

Any thing is instantaneous that is done at once, "occurring without any perceptible succession," "as the passage of electricity through any given space."

If the experience of heart purity is reached by a gradual process after conversion, it must be either by growth or by elimination by penance—for those who believe it is accomplished by death recognize it as an instantaneous work. If it is gradual by development, it is a contribution to the work of salvation by the addition of some element or quality that God intentionally omitted at conversion or was unable to supply. If it is by penance, it is a contribution to the work of salvation by the gradual removal from the soul of some unholy essence or quality which God intentionally left *in* the *soul* at conversion, or was unable to *eradicate* therefrom. Both these theories have their advocates; but a clear view of what constitutes entire sanctification and a limited knowledge of the laws of growth will demonstrate the impossibility of obtaining the experience in that way.

A primary and fundamental law of growth is "every thing after its kind," and six thousand years of recorded observation have produced no exception to this law. Growth is the gradual accumulation of such particles as now compose the animal or plant; and we have recently heard from Rev. Jos. Cook, in his Monday lectures, that "evolution and involution are always equal to each other." Hence there can be nothing evolved that is not first involved.

But the theory of completed salvation by growth is involved in another difficulty. Growth never changes the relation of things. Law gives precedence to the first occupant. Wheat is never sown in the forest to remove the underbrush and uproot the giant oaks. These occupy by right of inheritance. No instance of displacement by growth is on record in the history of the world. For years after the forests have been felled the stumps of massive trees remain in the best cultivated fields, scarred and blackened by the laborer's hand, demonstrating the fact that the growth of the most valuable crops by the most careful tillage can never eradicate the roots of the ancient forests.

Sin is indigenous in the soul by nature,—it has precedence. Sin has the ascendency in the heart by natural descent, and we could as easily displace the Norwegian forests by introducing the fragrant magnolia from the banks of the Mississippi, or extirpate the dense forests of North America by transplanting to its midst the stately palm from the Oriental empire, as we could grow sin from its native soil by the introduction of exotic graces. However vigorous may be the growth of spiritual life, if sin remain in the soul at conversion, even in a suppressed state, it can never be grown out.

If sin cannot be grown out of the soul, is it any more philosophical to suppose we can wear it out by ascetic rites and austere ceremonies ? by purgatorial flames or penal agonies? This theory has its advocates in all lands and among all classes. How shall I get rid of my sin ? asks the devotee of his priest at the shrine of Paganism ; drive your sandals full of spikes and walk five hundred miles over the sandy wastes, replies his priest. How shall I be sanctified and fitted for heaven ? asks the average Christian of to-day ; patiently endure all the afflictions God sends upon you, replies the average spiritual adviser of the period. A single quotation from one of the most popular preachers of this age will illustrate the extent to which this theory is ingrained into our beliefs :—"Before the wrought iron can become steel it must be heated by means of charcoal, and made to pass through a process of cementation, until it is blistered by fire and freed from a portion of its carbon ; and then the merciless hammer must complete the work. Before the coal gas, that at night illumines and beautifies the city, is fit for use, it must be freed from carbonic acid, tar, resinous compounds and other *impurities* which *dim* its *brilliancy;* and this is accomplished by first subjecting it to an intense heat and then passing it through water, cooling it in condensers, and transmitting it through tubes and purifiers. And just so it is with the growth and *spiritual progress* of the *soul.* The *friction* and *attrition*, the purging and purifying— the *heating* and *cooling. The sinning* and *repenting* to which we are *subjected*, the very *difficulties* and *painful* experiences we have to encounter, and of which we are so apt to complain, are the *necessary* conditions of our spiritual progress.''

But we affirm that sinning and suffering are not necessary conditions of spiritual progress, but that as sin has in itself all the elements by which it diffuses itself and becomes universal, so also does the atonement of Jesus Christ possess in itself all the agencies by which sin is to be destroyed. Pain is a product of sin. Sin cannot heal itself; therefore physical suffering is not a factor in the salvation of the world, but, on the contrary, is something that is to be destroyed.

The assumption that we are to expiate our own guilt, suffer out the penalty of violated law, and thus procure our own cleansing, is not only without authority of Scripture, but is a direct encroachment upon the work of the Lord Jesus Christ, for it is an assumption that our sufferings are meritorious or that they supersede the operation of the Holy Ghost. The conception of gaining salvation by suffering is one of the oldest forms of idolatry. It was incorporated into the Latin church from Pagan Rome, and has propagated itself with greater or less distinctiveness among all creeds and classes. It has dragged its bloody trail across four thousand years of the world's history, and to-day it stands beside Christian altars and with insulting mien challenges the blood of the Crucified One. We oppose both these theories because they divide the work of salvation, leaving only part for God to do, thereby making Christ only a partial Saviour, and offering to a sinful race an imperfect salvation, assuming that man being but partly fallen needs but little divine help.

But we affirm that the work of complete salvation or sanctification is instantaneously wrought in the soul by the Holy Ghost. However slow may be the preparation,—however tortuous the pathway of approach, when we come to the work of entirety, that is wrought at once, and is without perceptible succession.

But there is another line of approach to this question. If sin is an instantaneous act, salvation must be an instantaneous process. We all concede sin to be an act in which there is no perceptible succession, hence the results of sin upon the moral qualities of the soul must be instantaneous.

However slowly Adam and Eve approached the fatal act, however insidious the process of temptation, the culmination was sudden—guilt ensued at once. Spiritual death was as complete when God was excluded from the soul and Satan was admitted as physical death would be were every drop of blood extracted and the vascular system infused with prussic acid, and the corruption of the soul was complete in an instant.

During the six thousand years of the world's rebellion nothing has excelled the audacity with which Adam confronted his maker when dragged from his hiding-place. Turning like a base coward against her whom God had given him and whose honor was entrusted to his keeping, and by a legitimate inference hurling into the face of Jehovah the charge of complicity. "The woman *thou* gavest me, she is the cause of all this ruin."

Adam as effectually charges God with the responsibility of his fall as his degenerate children of this age who assume that sin is an essential factor in the government of God.

The defilement of the moral nature was *not* a gradual process. When Satan entered he seized every organ and diffused himself through every tissue and fibre of soul and body. This temple of God so suddenly defiled became the habitation of every unholy and vile thing.

The process of salvation, the perfect renovation of the soul, the restoration of the race to a state of perfect harmony with God, the complete restoration of all the relations with Him, and of all the moral qualities of His nature to the soul must be a reversal of the process by which the ruin was accomplished.

There must first of *all* be given the *full consent* of the party that God shall come in; there must be rendered a willing obedience to all His commands and requirements.

When we fulfil the conditions God pardons at once, the Holy Ghost comes in and quickens the soul into new life, and as suddenly as Satan defiled our moral nature by his unholy presence, God restores the perfect purity to our moral nature when He has permission to wholly possess us. Let the believing soul come as perfectly into sympathy with Christ as the unregenerate soul is with evil, and surrender as perfectly to the influence of the Holy Ghost as the ungodly does to the spirit of the world, and as suddenly as the unrestrained atmosphere will fill a vacuum God will come in and the soul will have an instantaneous experience of sanctification—an experience of purification in which there is no perceptible succession.

The phraseology of the Bible supports this view, it assures us that Jesus came to "save his people from their sins," to "cleanse them from *all* unrighteousness," that "the blood of Jesus Christ, his Son, cleaseth us from *all* sin;" that "He is able to save to the uttermost all that come unto God by him." It nowhere speaks of salvation by growth; no intimation is given of salvation by suffering; the Bible gives no account of a gradual salvation by any process whatever, but constantly announces to a world of perishing sinners, " Behold, *now* is the accepted time ; behold, now is the day of salvation."

The Scripture is as specific in its statement that Jesus is the source of purity as it is that He is the fountain of life. The Old Testament and the New agree. The Prophet says, " Then will *I* sprinkle clean water upon you and ye *shall* be *clean* from all your filthiness, and from all your idols will *I cleanse you.*" And when John was on the island of Patmos, and the heavens were opened, and his ears saluted with celestial music, he heard the multitude in the raptures of song declare that they " had *washed* their *robes* and made them *white* in the blood of the Lamb."

We may put this argument in another form. Sanctification is a part of our salvation. Jesus is our Saviour, and our salvation is His work. Whatever He undertakes as exclusively His work, He does at once. When Lazarus had lain in the grave four days, Jesus came and bade him come forth, and the dead obeyed. He touched the bier and gave to the desolate widow her son perfectly restored. He said to the blind man, " Receive thy sight," and immediately flooded his soul with perfect radiance. He said to the leper, "I will, *be thou clean.*" And instantly surprised him with perfect health.

This Jesus is " made unto us wisdom, righteousness, sanctification and redemption." He it is that has undertaken to purify our moral nature, and it must be without perceptible succession, for He is an instantaneous worker. In the beginning, " He spake, and it was done ; he commanded, and it stood fast." He stood upon the empty void, and dipping His finger in His own glory, touched the heavens and left them studded with innumerable worlds of beauty and light. " He breathed into man's nostrils the breath of life, and he became a living soul." " Jesus Christ, the same yesterday, and to-day, and forever." The Saviour of men, able at once to open spiritual eyes,—to lay His hand on the spiritual bier, and impart new life to the dead soul,—to speak to the moral leper, and make him entirely clean.

The argument may be summarized as follows :

Sin is an instantaneous act, and the moral consequences immediately follow the overt act. Complete Salvation is an instantaneous work wrought in the soul, and its various experiences do correspond with that operation. Guilt is an instantaneous result, following actual sin. Peace is an instantaneous result of actual pardon. Spiritual death was an instantaneous result of sin. Spiritual life as a conscious experience, is an instantaneous result of positive regeneration. The corruption of the soul as a result of sin was an instantaneous experience.

Hence the sanctification of the soul, which is the cleansing away of this inherited defilement, by the Holy Ghost, must be a work in which there is no perceptible succession.

We have the universal experience of the Christian world in evidence, that pardon and regeneration are experiences without perceptible succession, and we conclude that instantaneousness is God's method, so far as those processes of salvation are involved.

We have also the recorded testimony of thousands who have died in the triumphs of full salvation, and thousands of living witnesses who now enjoy the blessing of heart purity, who, all with one accord, affirm that they were cleansed from their sins by the blood of Jesus Christ as an instantaneous experience ; and the Evangelist records the testimony of the Church triumphant. He beheld a great multitude that no man could number, composed of the saved of all ages, all classes, all nationalities, and comprehending all the various periods of time, who all with one voice declared that " Jesus washed them from their sins in His own blood.'' And as washing is an instantaneous process, we infer that their cleansing was an experience not marked by successive stages.

We have therefore the direct Scripture statements,—the argument from philosophy. And the verdict of universal experience that entire sanctification is an instantaneous work wrought in the soul by the operation of the Holy Ghost.

We may put the argument into a logical form as follows :

Entire sanctification is the experience of complete salvation. Salvation is accomplished by God alone. Therefore it is neither by growth nor penance.

Salvation is a free gift bestowed upon the trusting soul by the Lord through the merit of Jesus Christ. The act of giving, whether conditional or arbitrary, is an act without perceptible succession ; hence sanctification is an experience instantaneously received.

On motion the Conference adjourned, after the doxology, and benediction by Bro. S. D. Clayton of Urbana.

---

*Third Day—Afternoon.*

After devotional exercises, a paper prepared and sent by Bro. C. A. Van Anda, of Rochester, N. Y., was read by Bro. C. W. Ketcham, P. E., of the West Cincinnati District, on the subject:

## TO WHAT EXTENT MAY WE BE SAVED FROM SIN IN THIS LIFE ?

### REV. C. A. VAN ANDA, D.D.

THE Word of God forbids all kinds and degrees of sin. Both the Hebrew and the Greek express sin by a term which means to err from, or miss the mark.

The Hebrew word is *yachate*, and is used to describe the accuracy with which the seven hundred chosen men of Benjamin could sling stones,—"Every one could sling stones at a hair breadth and not *miss.*"

The Greek word is *Amartia*, and is used by Greek writers as descriptive of a traveler's missing his way.

In the Scriptures God requires a certain standard of character and conduct, viz. : holiness and righteousness. This standard all have missed, and hence these terms to represent sin are applied both to the character and conduct of men. As to character it is said (Rom. 5 : 12), "Wherefore as by one man *sin* entered into the world." "That is," says Dr. Whedon, "Adam's disobedience, subordinated the good to evil in his moral constitution, and that changed moral state was transmitted to his posterity, according to a universal law of the entire generative kingdoms, vegetable, animal, and human, viz : " Like nature begets like nature."

Again, these terms are used to represent disobedience to God's law.

Thus, (1 John, 3: 4) "Sin is the transgression of the law."

The Scriptures condemn both the sinful *state* and the sinful *act*.

No kind or degree of sin, *properly so called*, is allowed in the word of God. Take any term descriptive of a sinful disposition, tendency or action, and it will be found that the Bible condemns that sin.

These terms are often unqualified, or, for example, "If I sin then Thou makest me, and Thou wilt not acquit me from mine iniquity." Here there is no qualifying term either for sin or iniquity, hence whatever is sin or iniquity is embraced.

Or take the following : "Sin is a reproach to any people," *i. e., sin* as such ; of any kind or degree.

Furthermore, there are cases where these and similar words are qualified by absolute terms. Take as an example, Rom. 1: 18, " For the wrath of God is revealed from heaven against *all* ungodliness and unrighteousness of men."

This argument is supported by all those scriptures which enjoin the *entire separation* of God's people from sin. Thus, 2 Cor., 6: 14-18 ; 7: 1, "Be ye not unequally yoked together with unbelievers; for what fellowship hath righteousness with unrighteousness? And what communion hath light with darkness?

And what concord hath Christ with Belial? or what part hath he that believeth with an infidel?

And what agreement hath the temple of God with idols? for ye are the temple of the living God ; as God hath said, I will dwell in them, and walk in them ; and I will be their God, and they shall be my people.

Wherefore come out from among them and be ye separate, saith the Lord and touch not the unclean thing ; and I will receive you. * * * Having therefore these promises dearly beloved, let us cleanse ourselves from all filthiness of the flesh and spirit, perfecting holiness in the fear of God."

The law of God is so exceedingly broad as to include even sins of ignorance.

In the fourth chapter of Leviticus, there is a special enactment against sins of ignorance, whether committed by one of the people, by a priest or by the whole congregation.

Jesus declares that the servant which knew not his Lord's will and yet did commit things worthy of stripes, should nevertheless be beaten, though with few stripes.

And even the expression, "the times of this ignorance God *winked at*," (Acts, 17: 30) does not teach that God can ever be indifferent to idolatry ; but simply that the Athenians, with only the light of nature, were under less obligations, than after the gospel was preached to them.

What has been said upon this point may be thus summarized :

God will not condemn men for either being, or doing, what they can by no possibility avoid ; He does condemn all sinful

4

character, and all sinful conduct; it must be therefore that we may be saved from all sin.

Again, the word of God requires *all righteousness; i. e.*, the presence in the soul of all the elements necessary to a complete righteousness of character ; and those elements unmixed, unalloyed, with anything contrary thereto, together with an outward life which is the fruit of this righteous character.

Take any term which stands for a righteous state, disposition or act of the mind, or for any righteous external action, and it will be found that God requires that state or action, up to the measure of our ability.

For example, a penitence free from impenitence—a godly sorrow for sin ; a simple faith, unmixed with unbelief; a love for God, the quality of which is expressed by the language, "with all thy heart, and with all thy soul, and with all thy mind, and with all thy strength." And a love for our neighbor, measured by the phrase, *"As thyself."*

I am not acquainted with any scripture which either directly, or by fair implication, allows, in a responsible being, the absence of any element essential to a completely holy character ; or of a course of conduct essential to a complete devotion to God.

In a word, God requires the presence of all the elements essential to holiness ; a devotion of all qualities, attributes, acquisitions and possibilities of being to Himself.

This position is sustained by such scriptures as : " Whether ye eat therefore or drink, or whatsoever ye do, do all to the glory of God."

" Put on therefore, as the elect of God, holy and beloved, bowels of mercies, kindness, humbleness of mind, meekness, long-suffering ; forbearing one another, if any man have a quarrel against any ; even as Christ forgave you, so do ye ; And above all these put on charity, which is the bond of perfectness, And let the peace of God rule in your hearts, to the which also ye are called in one body ; and be ye thankful."

And " Let the word of Christ dwell in you richly in all wisdom ; teaching and admonishing one another in psalms and hymns and spiritual songs, singing with grace in your hearts to the Lord. And whatsoever ye do, in word or deed, do all in the name of the Lord Jesus."

God cannot require anything beyond our possibility ; but He does require righteousness of character, and of conduct, therefore we may · be so saved from sin as to obtain a clean heart, and be preserved blameless unto the coming of our Lord Jesus Christ.

We are led to the same conclusion by the definition of terms used in the holy scriptures as descriptive of the character and life required of men.

In calling attention to a few of these terms let us observe the following rule :—Descriptive terms, unless restricted by their customary use, by their connection or by some limiting term, may be taken in their widest sense.

For example, if a Chemist should say of water which he had carefully analyzed, "it is pure," we would understand him to declare that there was no foreign substance in it.

If he were to add such a limiting word as entirely, perfectly or the like, there would be but one sense in which he could be understood.

Take the Hebrew term *Tamam*, to complete, to perfect, to finish.

See an instance of its use in Gen. vi. 9, " Noah was a just man, *perfect* in his generations."

The LXX render this term by Τελειος, *Telios*, from Τελειω, *Telio*, to complete or finish. The same term is used by the New Testament writers to denote the completion or end of anything.

Take the term *Kastesh*, that which is pure, holy, clean, sacred ; equivalent to the Latin *sanctus*.

It is often used to represent the state of a person and is

applied to one who consecrates himself to God. The verb, of course, means to make holy, to sanctify, to hallow.

Thus of the Sabbath, Gen. ii. 3, "And God blessed the seventh day and *sanctified* it." And so of persons, as in Deut. xx. 8, "I am the Lord which *sanctify* you." The LXX. render it by a term which means to make holy, to make clean from pollution. The same is true of New Testament writers, as in John x. 36, "Say ye of him whom the Father hath sanctified,&c.,"representing the sacredness of the mission of Jesus. And so of 1 Thess. v. 23, "And the very God of peace *sanctify* you wholly."

If we carefully examine the nature of the mission of Jesus Christ into the world, that examination will confirm the argument from the terms just examined.

The standard both for the character and conduct of men is holiness; but the carnal mind is enmity against God; it is not subject to the law of God, neither indeed can be. How is such a nature to be made holy? How is such a being to keep a holy law?

The answer is, through Jesus Christ our Lord. Jesus became a perfect man, was made under the law, fulfilled all righteousness, and died for the transgressors of the law; having such an abundance of merit, that His death as completely vindicates the Divine Justice, and magnifies and makes honorable the law, as it would have been if the original transgressor had perished. At the same time a new dispensation is ushered in, and humanity is no longer under the law, but under grace. That is to say, perfect obedience to the law is not now the condition of salvation; indeed, it never was to a sinner. In every case the justification of a sinner is through faith, faith being counted for righteousness, *i. e.* for perfect obedience to the law.

To trust in Christ, to love and obey up to the full measure of our present capacity, is as acceptable from us, as perfect obedience would have been from Adam, or from an angel. Yet this is neither Adamic, nor Angelic, but Christian perfection. This is the teaching of Rom. 8 : 1–4, "There is therefore now no condemnation to them which are in Christ Jesus, who walk not after the flesh but after the Spirit. For the law of the Spirit of life in Christ Jesus hath made me free from the law of sin and death. For what the law could not do in that it was weak through the flesh, God sending his own Son in the likeness of sinful flesh, and for sin, condemned sin in the flesh that the righteousness of the law might be fulfilled in us, who walk not after the flesh, but after the Spirit."

And the same is taught by Rom. 13 : 8–10, "Owe no man anything but to love one another: for he that loveth another hath fulfilled the whole law. * * * Love worketh no ill to his neighbor: therefore love is the fulfilling of the law."

A mistake of judgment, and consequently of feeling and of action ; a less amount of service than an unfallen being would render, is not sin properly so called.

A wounded soldier, clinging to the colors, and bearing them as far toward the front as his waning strength will admit, thereby gives as full an exhibition of patriotism, as if without a scar, he had planted them inside the enemies' works.

The same conclusion is reached by the argument from experience.

Any degree or kind of knowledge, no matter how obtained, is an experience. Thus the farmer determines the nature of his soils by certain tests or experiments. Hence he knows by *experience* what to plant, as, also, the season of planting, and the kind of cultivation needed to produce the best harvest.

Says McCosh: "Every conviction, be it of sense or consciousness, of the understanding, or of conscience, is an experience."

Pain from a wound, pleasure from eating food, or from viewing a landscape,—all these are experiences.

This argument involves two questions: (1) the reliability of religious experience, and (2) that of human testimony. We only know the experience of another through his testimony.

Is salvation from sin a matter of human experience? May we acquire the knowledge of salvation? If so, then to deny that any one is wholly saved from sin is to assume that we are acquainted with all kinds and degrees of religious experience as made known by testimony, and have thoroughly analyzed all testimony in support of such experiences, and have found it unreliable, since, if there is an experience unknown to us, or a testimony not proved unreliable, that experience may be that of salvation from all sin.

An exercise or state of the mind, or fear, joy, or peace, assurance, etc., etc., is as real, as certain, as our sensations produced by contact with material bodies; and testimony concerning the one class of experiences is as readily accepted as that concerning the other. The various affairs of life are carried on through our confidence in such testimony.

The same is true of religious experience and testimony. Is guilt and shame experienced when a parent or magistrate is disobeyed? The same is true when God is disobeyed. Is there peace and joy when the parent or magistrate pardons the transgressor? And may we be conscious of all this? Why not equally so when God pardons?

If we say all pain is gone, no one doubts our experience or our testimony. Why should there be doubt if we say all guilt and sin is removed?

If a true mother declares she has a love for her child in which there is no mixture of hatred, no one doubts either her experience or testimony. Why should we hesitate to receive her testimony as conclusive in the one case any more than in the other? That is to say, if she testifies that she loves God with all her heart, must we not receive her testimony as readily as when she declares she loves her child with all her heart? The faculty of love is the same, whatever is its object. If the exercise of this faculty is something of which we are conscious in one case, it is equally so in another.

The Bible is a safe guide in mental as well as in moral science, and without doubt these views are taught there. See an example in Psalm xxxii. 3–5 : "When I kept silence, my bones waxed old, through my roaring all the day long. For day and night thy hand was heavy upon me: my moisture is turned into the drought of summer.

"I acknowledged my sin unto thee, and mine iniquity have I not hid. I said, I will confess my transgressions unto the Lord; and thou forgavest me the iniquity of my sin."

All know how abundant testimony upon this subject is. Let us call upon a few witnesses to testify as to their experience upon this subject. In the sixth chapter of Isaiah we have the Prophet's testimony of his experience of salvation from all sin. He had such a view of Deity as led him to cry: "Woe is me! for I am undone; because I am a man of unclean lips." Then a seraph flew to him, having a live coal in his hand, taken from off the altar. "And," says the Prophet, "he laid it upon my mouth, and said, Lo, this hath touched thy lips, and *thine iniquity is taken away, and thy sin purged.*"

St. Paul declares (Gal. ii. 20): "I am crucified with Christ: nevertheless I live; yet not I, but Christ liveth in me: and the life which I now live in the flesh, I live by the faith of the Son of God, who loved me, and gave himself for me."

St. John testifies (1 John iv. 17, 18): "Herein is our love made perfect, that we may have boldness in the day of judgment; because as he is, so are we in this world. There is no fear in love; but perfect love casteth out fear; because fear hath torment. He that feareth is not made perfect in love."

Passing to uninspired testimony, we find St. Ignatius giving thanks that he had been granted a *perfect love for God.*

John Fletcher testified: "I declare unto you in the presence of God the Holy Trinity, I am now dead indeed unto sin."

Carvosso says: "I then reviewed the full witness of the Spirit, that the blood of Jesus had cleansed me from all sin. I was emptied of self and of sin, and filled with God."

Dr. A. Clarke, writing to Mr. Wesley, says: "I regarded nothing, not even life itself, in comparison of having my heart cleansed from all sin; and I began to seek it with full purpose of heart." He advised with a local preacher, whom he had heard enjoyed the grace. "Soon afterward," he says, "while earnestly wrestling with the Lord in prayer, I found a change wrought in my soul."

Joseph Benson testifies: "I could do nothing but pray that I might be holy, even as He is holy * * * My soul was, as it were, let into God, and satiated with His goodness. He so strengthened my faith as to perfectly banish all my doubts and fears, and so filled me with humble, peaceful love, that I could and did devote my soul and body and health and strength to His glory and service."

Bishop Asbury says, "I live in patience, in purity, and in the perfect love of God."

Prof. T. C. Upham testifies: "I was distinctly conscious when I reached it. I was then redeemed by a mighty power, and filled with the blessing of perfect love."

Rev. Robert Curran, M. D., says: "In my case, the struggle against my unbelieving nature went on over two years; but when my faith laid hold on Christ as a complete Saviour from all sin, my soul leaped into the fullest liberty."

Similar testimonies could be adduced until the number would reach thousands. They are given by men and women from every condition in life. These witnesses would be deemed worthy to give testimony on questions of fact and of experience by any civil court in Christendom. Corresponding as they do with the word of God, and being confirmed by their blameless lives, we must accept them as proof that Jesus is able to save them to the *uttermost*, all that come unto God by Him.

Additional remarks were made by Brothers Brooks and Inskip.

The Committee on Fraternal Address to the Churches reported through their Chairman, Bro. Brooks:

## REPORT OF COMMITTEE ON FRATERNAL ADDRESS TO THE CHURCHES.

The National Holiness Conference, assembled in Cincinnati, Ohio, Nov. 27th to Dec. 2d, composed of Christian ministers and laymen interested in, and co-operating for, the promotion of the doctrine and experience of scriptural holiness among the people of God, would express devout gratitude to the Heavenly Father for the manifest grace and blessing that have attended their humble efforts in this Christian work.

We have an assured conviction that the present general and rapidly-extending holiness revival, which is now attracting the attention and engaging the interest of the Christian world, is the result of a most gracious divine visitation, in which the agency of the Holy Spirit is most evidently manifest. The evidences of this gracious and most cheering truth are seen in a constantly-growing holiness sentiment among God's children, in the multiplication of agencies for the promotion of the cause of holiness, and the consequent rapid progress of the work of holiness among the people of God, in the providential access which the holiness doctrine is gaining in the churches of our land, and in the quickened and purified life of many Christians whom God has raised up in

4*

the various evangelical denominations in this and other countries, to testify to this cherished truth of our holy Christianity. The fact which all these evidences make so manifest, viz., that the present gracious revival of holiness is of God, calls for most grateful mention and remembrance.

As a definite and succinct statement of the doctrine of entire sanctification, as believed and inculcated by us, we submit the following :

Entire sanctification is the purification of the heart from all sin by faith in the atonement ; is subsequent to conversion, and attested by the Holy Ghost. This we believe to be in harmony with the word of God and with the experience of His children.

We are possessed of an earnest and affectionate solicitude for the more extended and more rapid dissemination of the holiness doctrine, and for a more general and cordial acceptance of the experience by the children of God. We therefore kindly urge all who are co-workers in the holiness cause, to renewed and more zealous effort for its promotion. In a Christian movement so Catholic in spirit, and affording providential opportunities, so numerous and inviting, for rapidly and permanently advancing the cause of God, none need want for occasions or wait for invitations to labor. We trust that all the disciples of our Lord who have experienced the assured blessedness of perfect love, will engage to spread scriptural holiness over this whole land, and that they will, like the early disciples, be witnesses of this salvation wherever they go, " even to the uttermost parts of the earth."

We are persuaded of the equal importance and advantage of a faithful and loyal adherence, on the part of Christians who have experienced and are testifying to holiness, to the Churches with which they are respectively identified. If possessed of the grace of perfect love, they have, and must exhibit, the charity that " believeth all things, hopeth all things, endureth all things." And if faithfully and affectionately loyal to the Churches of which they are members, they will realize much advantage in the more cordial bearing of their brethren toward them as partakers of the same Church fellowship, and in the nearer and more welcome access they will find to the hearts of their fellow-members in their efforts to persuade and influence them to an acceptance of the same precious experience which they themselves enjoy.

We deem it important to call the attention of all who feel interested in the diffusion of holiness truth, to the necessity of patronizing, and, as far as possible, procuring circulation for, our holiness literature. For the advocacy of our holiness reform there are now issued, weekly and monthly, papers and periodicals, furnishing, it may be, an adequate supply of pure and reliable holiness reading for all demands of the present, or of the immediate future. While it is neither desired nor purposed, by the issue of these publications, to supersede the regular and authorized newspapers and periodicals that are published by the Churches, it is thought necessary to supply, in the way of special publication, the general and growing demand for strict holiness reading which exists among Christians. The necessity for such a provision to meet the demand spoken of, is apparent from the fact that the contents of the regular Church papers must necessarily be of a general and diversified character, and for this reason space cannot be given for any considerable amount of purely or exclusively holiness reading. Again we express our conviction of the importance of extending a generous patronage to our holiness publications.

Finally, we have much cause for thankfulness for our past success in our holiness work, and hopeful for successes to come. Let us wisely and faithfully use every means that the Lord approves for the promotion of this precious cause, and for the securing of its ultimate triumph. Let us do this with an humble conviction of our own insufficiency for the responsible work, and with a prayerful and trustful dependence upon the all-sufficiency of Almighty God and our Saviour Jesus Christ, to whom be all the glory of our salvation and our Christian work. Amen.

JOHN P. BROOKS,
GEO. D. WATSON,
W. McDONALD,  } *Committee.*
E. T. WELLS,

Which was adopted by unanimous vote.'

By vote, the Editors of religious papers were respectfully requested to publish the address; printed slips to be furnished the Secretaries to forward to the several papers.

Bro. Ketcham was respectfully requested to address the Conference on the subject: "The methods to be used and the proprieties to be observed in promoting the doctrine and experience of Christian Holiness."

After the doxology the benediction was pronounced by Bro. Ketcham.

---

*Friday Afternoon.*

At 7 o'clock the people gathered and spent half an hour in a precious season of prayer and song, after which the Conference was opened with prayer by Brother Thos. K. Doty, and then listened to a sermon from Brother Ricker, of upper Iowa, from the text Gal. 6: 9-10. At the conclusion of the sermon Brother Inskip exhorted fervently on the power of the blood to cleanse, and several came to the altar of prayer as seekers of heart purity. Adjourned with the benediction.

---

*Fourth Day.—Morning.*

After a prayer and experience meeting led by Brother Wm. McDonald, the Conference was formally opened; the minutes of yesterday were read and approved.

The order of the day was taken up, and Brother John P. Brooks, editor of the *Banner of Holiness*, read an essay on the subject :

## "WHAT ARE THE CHIEF HINDRANCES TO THE PROGRESS OF THE WORK OF SANCTIFICATION AMONG BELIEVERS?"

JOHN P. BROOKS, D.D.

In mentioning the hindrances to the holiness work, I instance, first, the circumstance of unaccessibleness to churches and communities. It is true, indeed, that the gospel of holiness has been widely proclaimed. Yet it is as true that there are many, very many places where it has not entered, at least in the form of settled or established ministration. To these excepted places, access in the sense named, has not yet been gained. The opportune time may not yet have come. Certainly, the door of access has not yet been providentially opened. For the most part, these unentered and unoccupied points are populous, prominent, influential. While some of them, in their relation to all religious and churchly enterprises, are important centers. I say, *for the most part*, because, whatever may be the explanation of the fact, it *is* a fact (at least, in the West, and I speak for the West, mainly), that the people, outside the more populous towns and cities—the country communities, the rural people—are readier and freer to hear, believe, and embrace the truth of holiness, than the populations *within* the cities. Not that the doctrine of holiness has not found entrance into some cities of population and influence, or that its preaching has not resulted in blessed fruitage there. The truth has gained, and is holding some such vantage positions. But commonly, the fact is as stated. The less populous (which are the more pious) communities, outside the great cities, are more tolerant toward holiness at the first, and more cordially in love with it at the last, than metropolitan people.   Our holiness reform, to reach the widest and most thorough results, demands open, unrestricted access to places and peoples.   Such access it has not had in the past; it has not at the present.   That it may have, *hereafter*, will depend much on the spirit of its champions,—upon the *wisdom* and *courage* shown in its propagation on the part of those who have been divinely commissioned for its advocacy.

A question that comes to us with an interest as amazing as momentous, is this—*why* is it that holiness—a doctrine so biblical and evangelical—a form of gospel inculcation so vital and so fundamental to our Christian experience and life—a divine truth that embodies so actually and savingly all that is essential and orthodox, both of doctrine and devotion, in our precious Christianity—*why is it* that holiness is looked upon with disfavor and disesteem by those who are called Christians—why is it that in its approach to peoples and Churches, it encounters checks and challenges, and is halted afar off until it can be questioned as to what it is and what it purposes, and at the end of all this withstanding, is often denied presence or place in the communities and Churches where it desires admission ?   However the question may be answered, the very fact to which the question alludes, stands as sadly and surely symptomatic of a weakened and deteriorated Christianity.

This question of *access*, in its relation to the diffusion of holiness, is of immense moment.   The work of introducing and establishing holiness cannot and must not cease because of the present unfriendly and opposed relation which many of the Churches sustain to that work.   It will not do for those who have come under solemn vows to God in the guidance of this great reform, even to halt, much less suspend their work because of expressed or manifested distaste to holiness, or dissatisfaction with holiness work or workers among the Churches. I believe in the providential possibility, and equally in our divine prerogative of *making access*, where it is not. Where entrance into new fields can be gotten without the asking, it ought to be taken. Where entrance can only be gained *by the* asking, it ought to be asked. Where entrance *has* not been secured, and *cannot* for the asking, then should entrance be procured *anyhow*, independent of all considerations and all conditions *but the command of God.*

A well-known holiness evangelist, in Illinois, said to me, in the course of a conversation, this, in purport : '' When I first set out in my evangelistic career, I determined to enter no place—city, town, or neighborhood, only as I was expressly invited by the pastor, (meaning the Methodist pastor, the evangelist himself being a Methodist). At the end of my first year, I modified my purpose, and resolved that I would myself ask the pastor for permission to enter his town. Still later, under divine leadings, I determined to ask *God's will only* as to my movements, and wherever a place of meeting could be secured, Church, school-house, public hall, or private residence, *there to go,* and in the name of God, set up the holiness banner." And in the light of this latest and best conviction, he is going forward to-day, spreading scriptural holiness over the land. And this, it seems to me, is and can be the only right and God-approved rule of procedure in our great work of holiness propagandism. I would not broach ecclesiastically any principles or plans of agrarianism. But I would recognize and abide by the expressed will of God, that His holy Gospel be universally promulgated, even to '' every creature." And I would hence insist upon the duty of every one to whom God has committed a dispensation of this precious gospel of full salvation, to procure for it as wide a hearing among men as a holy zeal and courage can secure, or the providences of God will allow.

I next speak of the unsympathy and non co-operation of Church agencies as constituting another hindrance, and as standing behind and being a principal occasion of the exclusion of holiness work and workers from the Churches. I simply submit as a fact (with unlimited proof in reserve), that the current Church sentiment of the times is decidedly at variance with the truth and spirit of holiness. For this reason, holiness is denied the sympathy and co-operation of the usual Church agencies, and to the precise extent of the withdrawal of such sympathy and co-operation, the work of holiness is hindered.

None who have stood identified with the holiness work, and have been actively engaged in its prosecution, during the last few years, can fail to know of the *general* unkindly disposition of the Churches toward themselves and the work in which they are engaged. They cannot have failed to observe that the Churches to which they would so gladly carry the precious tidings of a high and heavenly experience, are possessed of a certain adverse feeling toward them and toward the truth they minister, which renders their approach to the Churches often uncordial, and sometimes openly obnoxious. Such manifestations are plainly declarative of an alienated and opposed sentiment, which, however it may have come into existence, is seriously obstructive of the truth, and becomes a grievous trial to the meekness and patience of those who are God's commissioned proclaimers of this precious salvation.

It is perfectly obvious that this adverseness of Church sentiment on the subject of holiness, is to be attributed to some cause or causes. *Any* prevailing form of public sentiment, whether within or without the Church, does not come into existence independently. It is *produced*. It is *always* an effect. If we should look after the causes of this inimical Church sentiment, pervading as it does all divisions of the visible Church, we would find them distinctly various, yet all combining to the common result. In one view, we would be led to attribute the enmity to the influence of certain theological opinions, which, imbibed from *the creed*, have descended unchanged through the generations, inheriting all the doctrinal antipathies that were cherished by the fathers of the denomination, with no better reason for cherishing them than that the same were cherished by their fathers. The opposition to holiness in certain Churches, has *descended*. It has come down to the children from the fathers in the way of transmission through the teachings of *the creed*.

In another view, we would assign a pertinacious sectarian ism as the cause, which in its extreme forms becomes bigotry, and having become such, holds "THE CHURCH" above all else. To the bigoted sectarian, the love of Church becomes a superstition, himself becomes an idolater, "the Church" his idol. Thenceforth he seems not capable of any higher or holier devotion than that which is bestowed upon "the Church." The Wesleys, being in the midst of their reformation, admonished of the danger of the probable separation of the Societies from the Church, replied: "Church or no Church, *we* must attend to the work of saving souls. The church! we neither set it up, nor pull it down—but *we* must build the city of God." The ultra sectarian would reverse the sentiment—"Souls or no souls, we must attend to the work of saving *the Church*." The Churches are possessed with an opposed sentiment toward holiness, because of the essentially opposed animus of sectarianism.

Another account of this enmity would place the responsibility of it upon the ministers of the Churches. An adverse Church sentiment concerning holiness or any other specialty of Christian doctrine, might be looked for as a result when the pulpit is uncommitted for, or is decidedly committed against it. Notoriously, there are ministers not a few, who

are the authorized expounders of doctrine in the denominations for which they speak, who steadily and purposely ignore
the subject of holiness in their pulpit ministrations. Their
omission to teach holiness leaves their hearers uninformed,
and when "the Church" is in question, to be uninformed
touching Christian doctrine is to be averse to it. In such a
case, the unfriendly sentiment which exists is not so much a
purposed and pronounced hostility as an ignorant and indifferent antipathy.

Then there is set forth from some pulpits a certain diluted,
attenuated, emasculated species of popularly-adapted holiness
which carries with it no offence of the cross, and, for the same
reason, no savor of salvation from sin. It is an easy, indul-
gent, accommodating, mammonized kind of religion, whose
followers are given license, even though sanctified with the
sanctification that such pulpits enjoin, to become the abettors
of and partakers in a certain class of recreative and dissipative
practices that are so much in vogue in popular and carnal
Churches. I refer to Churchly social entertainments, the objective purport of which is to provide money for Church ex-
penses, substituting for conscience carnal policy, *and*, for the
increase of Church revenues, resorting to finesse to make good
the short-comings of a defective consecration. Church parties, suppers, festivals, lotteries, raffles, Sabbath concerts, tab-
leaux representations, pantomimic actings, dramatic persona-
tions, etc., etc., might head the catalogue of these *more* devil-
ish than doubtful devices. The pulpits that minister *such* a
holiness to their polite and worldly conformed congregations
—a holiness so largely without any grace of separation or self-
denial—a holiness so nearly crossless and Christless—are responsible in their measure for an opposed and prejudiced sentiment toward holiness. This is so because the doctrine of *true*
holiness, whenever attempting access to such carnalized
Churches, will prove so ultra in principle and so exacting in
practice that its introduction will be resisted to the last.

But still worse, if worse can be, there are pulpits, and many of them, from which holiness is declaimed against ; from some of them, misrepresented ; from others, berated ; from still others, calumniated. Utterances are continually coming to the public, from pulpit and press, carrying with them all the prestige of ministerial deliverance or endorsement, that reveal an animus of intense and relentless opposition to the holiness reform. Many of these deliverances are the more weighty, and become more influential in moulding and guiding public opinion, on account of the high official origin from which they proceed. "Where the word of a king is, there is power," says Solomon. The power attributed to the royal word may not be intrinsic to the word itself. It may be, indeed, an insignificant word, a weak word, an idle word, a *foolish* word. But, spoken by *the king*, it carries a power with it. Its potentiality follows from its royalty. The words that are spoken unkindly and untruly of the holiness movement by Christian ministers in high station carry with them a greater power of mischief than resides in the *mere* expression. They take importance, and become forcible from their rank. And because issuing from high places, they will find echo from other and humbler mouths; and repetitions innumerable will follow; for where there is fame there is flattery, and power is usually attended with parasitism.

A noticeable characteristic of this ministerial opposition to holiness is the disposition *to seem* unopposed, and an apparent unwillingness to accept the responsibility which an openly or avowedly opposed attitude would impose. For this reason it has come to be a part of anti-holiness tactics, &c., and to seem to resent every intimation or accusation that would identify them with the opposition. Here is a case in which, if actions do not speak louder than words, or words than actions, both words *and* actions declare with plainest emphasis a hostility which no affectation can conceal.

Another hindrance to the holiness work is found in the rigid and extreme denominationalism of our times. The Church becomes visible by becoming organic. It concretes itself in forms of polity. Each division of Christ's Church becomes peculiar, and is made distinctive by its own characteristic tenets, usages, and name. These differing sects have grown and are growing so numerous as to be almost countless. In how far these sectly contradistinctions are made necessary by the conditions of our society, or how far their multiplication has been pleasing to God, are questions that do not belong to this treatise. The fact of their existence I mention, that I may submit the other fact spoken of, viz. : that this spirit of denominationalism is more or less obstructive of our holiness work. In the nature of things, where co-existing organizations arise, aspiring to public influence and permanency of establishment, there must be rivalry. The conditions of their continuance, from a necessity that the very circumstance of co-existence involves, must be competitive. The sect, to survive, must not only live, but *grow*. And if it rise to a controlling rank and prestige, it must in its competitive relation to other living and growing sects, not only grow, but *outgrow*. With the spirit of rivalry that competitive struggle begets, there comes the danger of a lessened devotion, and in the end, a compromised spirituality. How these consequences ensue, I may not wait to explain. The thought I now aim at is this : The issue of these sectly rivalries is a rigid and extreme denominationalism.

Perhaps *this* thought may be questioned, and the fact to which it alludes, denied. Especially in the light of the recent sectarian advances, agreements, co-operative unities and fraternizations in Christian work, it may be insisted that the denominations, as to their mutual relations, are not so averse or alienated—that the churches are not so variant in their *moods*, as to sectarian sentiment, or their *modes*, touching their manner of working, as formerly. It is well known how this plea for a yielding and diminishing sectarianism would be urged. All know how this argument for a lately inaugurated and abounding catholicity would be carried out. It would be done in the way of reference to union platforms, union affiliations, union assemblies, union enterprises, union work, union successes, union congratulations and rejoicings, on account of Christ's advancing kingdom. Nor will it be denied that the reference is somewhat upheld by actual co-operative occurrences among the churches. *And*, that so much of union among Christian workers has transpired, is a cause of gladness and gratitude. But a close inquiry into the question of *essential* oneness of sentiment and feeling among the denominations would show how little of essential union has yet obtained, and how much has yet to be gained in order to demonstrate the real and vital oneness of the sects. Indeed, it could be easily shown that holiness *only* can, in any sense that is veritable and vital, unify the denominations, or rather, unify Christians. In point of fact, the "unity of the Spirit" is the *true* Christian unity. The Holy Spirit is the procurer of unity among Christ's people, and the holiness truth is *the* truth through which such unity is procured. "Sanctify them through Thy truth ... THAT they all may be one." Concerning what is called the union movements of the times, it is a characteristic and significant circumstance that the advances which the sects seem to be making toward each other present nothing of important concession.

Their agreements show nothing of surrender. Their co-operative performances reveal nothing of compromise as to what is characteristically and essentially distinctive. It is hardly at all in proof of a growing unsectarianness that in union assemblies, where various Churches meet, there is by consent an ignoring for the moment of sectish peculiarities, for the sake of a common cause, when it is known that what in such a case is called *union,* is agreed to by bringing into notice only what is non-essential in the estimation of the uniting Churches, and leaving out of notice all that is held as *essential* to their denominational character.   For Christians to meet and *resolve* that the Churches are one, when the enactment proceeds upon the understanding that each of the Churches *so resolving* surrenders *nothing,* but clings to *everything* that makes it distinctive and constitutes it *a sect,* may be an innocent and entertaining exercise enough, but it does not go a great way in demonstrating Christian unity.

As to the *spirit* of sectarianism, it is not less vital than heretofore.   The co-operative movements among the sects which seem to denote unity, denote not so much *that,* as a kind of sentimental toleration, a mutually agreed disposition to seem reciprocal by keeping out of view, in so far as is practicable, what is denominationally offensive, and putting up with sectish idiosyncrasies that cannot be hidden or repressed. After all this showing of agreed sentiment and agreed effort on the part of the denominations, it is yet true that each sect holds to its own distinctive creeds and forms  as tenaciously as ever, *and,* when these are attacked, will be found not less vigilant or valiant for their defence, in the present than in the past.

As to the later public union denominational movements, I think this remark may be offered truthfully and not uncharitably.   And the observation will show that such concerted movements are hardly so much in proof of *oneness* among Christ's people in matters of Christian belief and practice, as that the sects are as sectarian as ever.   The remark is this: where our Churches unite to forward a religious scheme, having reference either to local revival, or to general gospel propagandism, their participation in the movement is often (perhaps generally) prompted by some hope or prospect of sectarian advantage if the movement be entered into, or fears of sectarian *disadvantage* if the movement be not entered into.

The larger and leading sects become parties to the " union " effort, because of the opportunity the occasion affords to obtain added influence, and an enlarged control of public sentiment by co-operation, and their hope that out of the results that shall be developed from the movement, something may be secured of substantial advantage to themselves. The lesser and weaker sects fear to refuse participation in the " union " movement, because, already small and weak, and with circumscribed influence, it would be to their prejudice, as public sentiment goes, to withhold co-operation. The thought, too, and the hope that *something* of profit *may* come *to them*, who, because of their littleness, need even more than others, to reap advantage from the general results, persuades them to co-operation.

The *plain truth* is simply here : In its very nature the spirit of sectarianism is selfish. It lives for itself; it provides for itself; it prays for itself; it works for itself. And it stands against everything that in seeming or in fact antagonizes it. Holiness is held by the sects as in antagonism. First, because it is not in *the Creed.* Next, because it is feared as divisive in its tendencies. But principally because, by a prevailing misapprehension, it is held as itself sectarian. This last thought demands a little continued attention. Whatever holiness, as a form of doctrine or experience might be found to be, if historically examined, as to *denominational* identification and affinity, is not so important now. It is true, in point of fact, that holiness is generally regarded by the Churches as altogether Methodistical, as belonging to and characterizing Methodism in a sectarian sense. On account of this prevailing opinion, to attempt its advocacy or its introduction into the Churches is, in their view, to attempt to Methodize them, not by open capture, but by an indirect method of proselytism. Hence, all efforts that look to the indoctrination of the Churches on the subject of holiness *through Methodist agency*, are unwelcome, and often meet with a pronounced resistance at the outset. Despite this error, the light of holiness finds small apertures in the various *denominational* structures through which it steals its way, little crevices of entrance thro' which it shoots its brightening and cheering rays, and incarnating itself here and there in the experience and life of devout and simple-minded ones, becomes an illumination to others, a bright-shining candle upon the candlestick within the unlighted house.

This persuasion that misleads the Churches, viz.: that holiness is sectarian, that it is only.Methodism in a more insinuating form, is not altogether due to the denominational temper of those Churches, which *because* it is a sectarian temper, is ever wary and suspicious. It has been promoted by Methodists themselves. And *more*, by Methodists who are themselves interested in and laboring to advance the holiness cause. From very honest and well-meant conviction that holiness can be best propagated in the *Methodist* Church and among *Methodists* by enforcing the idea of its *Methodist* origin, and its distinctively *Methodist* authority and antecedents, the friends of holiness have themselves fallen into the error of holding and inculcating holiness as *Methodism*, and consequently as sectarian in its character and claims. In all this, an advantage may have been gained to *Methodism* in the higher authoritativeness with which the doctrine of holiness when thus enforced comes to *Methodists*. But it is a question whether there does not result a *more* than counterbalancing disadvantage in the sectarian prejudices on the part of other denominations which such distinctively sectarian appeals are adapted to beget. The *right* to do this, that is to appeal to *Methodists* as under obligation to accept holiness because holiness is itself *Methodism*, may not be questioned —the propriety of it, for reasons here mentioned, *may*. The *lawfulness* of such enforcements may be granted, but the *ex-*

*pediency* of them may not be so apparent. It would seem wise, as to expediency, and just, as to all the considerations of equity involved, to hold forth and enforce holiness as an altogether Catholic doctrine—*Catholic*, because belonging in the sense of property to *no one sect*, but to all—*Catholic*, because coming to the people of God more from the general Gospel than from the catechism, more from the Bible than the discipline. Thus, standing forth, as I think the holiness doctrine should, clothed with the garb of an obvious and acknowledged catholicity, it could approach the Churches with its persuading and convincing overtures with less liability to rejection, and with a more reasonable trust of general welcome hearing and cordial acceptance. And upon the principles of unsectarian advocacy which are here submitted and argued for, *Methodist* holiness workers should be most free and forward to invite and cherish fellowship with all holiness workers in other denominations, and to accept them as fellow-helpers in one precious Gospel by joining them in all public efforts to advance holiness, and by inviting them, with glad and cordial recognition of their experience and their gifts, to a participation in and co-operation with all our public, general holiness movement.

Still another hindrance to holiness is found in the declined piety of all the Churches. I know the sensitiveness of the general Christian mind touching anything like inquiry into the religious state of the Churches, and particularly, when there seems to be on the part of those proposing the inquiry, an implied conviction of general deficiency and short-comings in piety. But no carnal sensitiveness on the part of formal and proud-hearted Christians should deter inquiry into the general state of religion, and a righteous exposure of what is evil in the Churches. For the last third of a century, expressions like the following have been coming to the public. I quote the sayings of revered men of different denominations :

5

From J. A. James, Congregationalist: "What is the present spiritual condition of the great bulk of the professors of religion? We behold a strange combination of zeal and worldly-mindedness; great activity for the extension of religion in the earth, united to lamentable indifference to the state of religion in the soul. In short, *apparent vigor in the extremities, with a growing torpor at the heart!* The Christian profession is sinking in its tone and piety. The line of separation between the Church and the world becomes less and less perceptible, and the character of genuine Christianity as expounded *from pulpits* and delineated in books, has too rare a counterpart in the lives and spirit of its professors."

From J. C. Ryle, Episcopalian: "Surely no man, with his eyes open, can fail to see that the Christianity of the New Testament is something far higher and deeper than the Christianity of most professing Christians. That formal, easy-going, do little thing, which most people call *religion*, is evidently not the religion of the Lord Jesus."

From H. C. Fish, Baptist: "The piety of the present day has widely degenerated from the divine standard."

From Stephen Olin, Methodist: "The Church is now barely able to hold its ground against the opposing forces of sin and error, or to advance with tardy step to future triumphs. And if it is to be recruited and reinforced ONLY by *such members and ministers* as already wield its destinies, it must remain in essentially the same condition."

Said Harris, of England, "THE CHURCH ITSELF REQUIRES CONVERSION."

Kincaid, the missionary, declared, "To the great Head of the Church WE MUST LOOK FOR A NEW ORDER OF CHRISTIANS, Christians just as absorbed in winning souls to Christ, as worldlings are in gathering gold."

A whole hour's time could be taken up with like sentiments, quoted from respectable and authoritative sources.

But time forbids me to dwell on this thought. What I say must be briefly said. The bane of the Churches is the carnal spirit that is in them. And this spirit is with them and in them. It dwells in and controls them all. Carnal preachers stand in carnal pulpits, and preach carnal sermons to carnal hearers, who sit with carnal ease to hear, and then go out with carnal desires and carnal purposes to live a carnal life. To such, the Bible standard of piety—holiness—is *in heart* disliked, and *in life* disowned. Carnal religionists, with whom the churches *are filled*, do not wish to accept in their faith, or adopt in their lives, the Bible rule of holiness. Immense numbers of church members hate holiness, do not wish or aim to be holy, because the Lord their God is holy, perfect, even as their Father in heaven is perfect. They deny intellectually and practically the possibility, and even the practical importance of obedience to the divine command, "Be ye holy." They love sin. They wish to live in it. They *intend* to do so. And so their lives are, as matter of fact, lives of sinful indulgence. They live as though God did not require or expect them to be holy. This carnal spirit *controls* in the churches. It erects gorgeous and costly temples, to gratify its pride. It calls preachers who will minister to its worldly tastes and practices. It seeks the favor and suffrage of the rich and great, for their wealth and reputation's sake, rather than for the sake of their souls. It "*runs*" the churches by means of carnal arts and appliances, looking more to worldly approval than to godly worship, more to man-pleasing than to God-serving, more to secular success than to spiritual enlargement, more to gain than godliness. It is only to know what holiness is, to know that it does and *must* antagonize at every point, this man pleasing, world-loving, mammon-serving sort of piety. That in such carnalized churches there should be a distaste for holiness, and a united rising up to resist its approach, is altogether what would be expected. "For what fellowship hath righteousness with unrighteousness, and what communion hath light with darkness, and what concord hath Christ with Belial, or what part hath he that believeth with an infidel, and what agreement hath the temple of God with idols?" So long as there remains in the churches this unrighteousness and darkness, and so long as carnal counsels prevail in and rule over the churches, so long will the doctrine of holiness be held aloof, and so long will its witnesses be discountenanced and proscribed.

&. I have thus spoken of these several hindrances to the holiness work. The view so taken is wholly objective. These hindrances are all exterior to holiness itself. There *are* hindrances, also, that accompany our holiness work, that are interior to the movement itself. A glance at these—a *mere* glance—and my task is done.

1. Imperfect teaching. Holiness to be known must be taught. Those whom the Lord appoints to the work, must teach others. But it is to be feared that some are attempting to teach whom God has not appointed. To teach a truth and a doctrine so important *as holiness,* is a highly responsible undertaking. Not *every one* is equal to its requirements or its responsibilities. It is becoming, I fear, *too much* of a persuasion with holiness people (and the persuasion may not *always* come of Him who calleth them), that, because *they* have experienced a deliverance so blessed and joyous, they are therefore made capable of becoming public teachers to others concerning the precious grace. Not necessarily is this so. Every possessor of a holy experience is a competent and qualified *witness,*—but not necessarily a competent and qualified teacher. In so far as holiness is represented and inculcated *doctrinally,* IN THE WAY OF public teaching, by those who possess no natural or gracious aptness as instructors, and whose teachings must hence be crude and imperfect,

perhaps essentially incorrect, the cause must suffer. And that it has suffered in such a way I have no doubt.

2. Unthorough experiences. In our holiness work we find some who, professing the experience, do not present the inward and outward evidences of a veritable sanctification. Perhaps this circumstance results somewhat from the matter just noticed, viz. : imperfect teaching. At any rate, the evil exists, and holiness suffers from it. When persons profess holiness without possessing it, the doctrine suffers by the necessary misrepresentation of the holiness truth which their unsanctified lives imply. Some persons, in the matter of holiness as in the matter of justification, and not a few, *do this*, and, regarded by the Church and the world as being representative of holiness, while their lives are inconsistent and unholy, holiness stands compromised, and loses influence. This is a hindrance.

3. A form of holiness that is unaggressive and inert. *Such* a holiness is sometimes seen. Of course, it is a holiness of intrinsically spurious quality. Or else, if ever genuine, it is *now* but a *form* of holiness from which the *power* has died away. Some holiness people answer to this description. Some holiness meetings, (stated meetings, I mean,) do. They go on, month after month, year after year, professing holiness and *doing nothing* for holiness. They are passively good, inertly innocent—but without *power* —"DEAD unto sin," possibly, but *certainly* NOT "alive unto God." The Church and community where such people live are impressed that holiness is a spiritless, forceless thing, that has no inspiration of active well-doing in it. Such a holiness is in the way. It is a hindrance.

4. Unedifying and misleading testimonies. We encounter these. Some say—"I am not tempted"—"I *cannot* sin"— "I am infallibly saved, I *cannot fall.*" All these testimonies are untrue, misleading, and mischievous. They work harm to the holiness cause and are a hindrance.

5. A temptation to Church unaffiliation. The Churches do not receive holiness ; many pastors dislike and some *forbid* the holiness testimony. Those in the experience see that neither the Church nor the pastor commends, sympathizes with, or appreciates them. And sometimes both the pastor and the Church act as if they did not *want* them. The temptation is immediate—" leave the Church." Sometimes the temptation prevails, but it ought not. Then again, those in the experience of holiness see so much and are brought into contact with so much in the Church that, with the light given them, they know to be wrong and wicked, that they feel at times the temptation—"*leave the Church.*" Some yield to the temptation. But they should not. Holiness people need the Church, and even if they did not *the Church* needs the holiness people. This centrifugal tendency should be withstood.

6. Excessive and extravagant experiences. These accompany religion, in every form of experience. They accompany though not involved in, or resultant from, holiness. No doubt they come of Satan. Perhaps *sometimes*, from a partially disordered brain. Under their influence, persons are led to say and do things that are illegitimate, extravagant, sometimes wicked. But it must be remembered that these experiences which lead to excess, and in the end, it may be, *to sin*, ARE NOT HOLINESS EXPERIENCES. Holiness is not in any true or just sense, identified with them, and *will not* be responsible for them. Yet they appear, and no doubt will, so long as the devil can succeed in making out of nervous-sanguine professors who are Christians, or who are not Christians, *fanatics*. But these clairvoyant and religiously cataleptic people hinder the holiness work.

Remarks were made by Brothers Inskip, McDonald, and Ricker.

Adjourned with benediction by Brother Wilson.

*Fourth Day.—Afternoon.*

The customary devotional exercises were held in opening, Brother Murray of Oxford, O., leading in prayer.

Minutes of the morning read and approved.

By vote, Brother Brooks was requested to preach on Sabbath at 3 o'clock, P. M., in the absence of Brother J. A. Wood.

The order of the day was taken up, and the Conference heard an essay by Brother Wm. T. Perkins on the question; "What is the duty of the laity of the Church in view of the present interest upon the subject of holiness?"

Additional remarks were made by Brothers Inskip and Mc-Donald.

Brother C. W. Ketcham read an essay on

## "METHODS TO BE USED, AND THE PROPRIETIES TO BE REGARDED IN SPREADING SCRIPTURAL HOLINESS THROUGHOUT THE LAND."

### REV. C. W. KETCHAM.

Not knowing who suggested this theme, nor for what special reasons it is before us, I think it fair to premise that it springs from the purest of motives, and the most sincere desire to please God and subserve the best interests of the Church.

But in consenting to introduce the subject, I must not be understood as undertaking an elaborate investigation, or by any means to notice all the points that may legitimately have near or remote connection with it.

This subject, embracing as it does, the life-work of the ministry, the health and success of the Church, and eventuating in the salvation of myriads of souls, or otherwise, cannot fail to awaken the deepest interest in a Methodist Preachers' Meeting; unless the vows of God sit lightly upon us, and our call to the ministry is held to be a phantom of the past, or a mere Churchly farce.

The statement of the subject precludes discussion as to the nature of holiness, or what it is, as that is considered among the things settled, or at least unquestioned, and unquestionable, so far as this inquiry is concerned.

It evidently assumes :

1. That "holiness" is a doctrine explicitly taught and enjoined in God's word.

2. That it is attainable, may be lived and enjoyed in contact with the rugged realities of business life, by the average Christian, or the great body of believers. Otherwise there would be no motive for seeking to spread it among the people.

3. That it is not only sanctioned by the highest teaching of God's word, but that it is conceded to be distinctively a doctrine of the Methodist Episcopal Church.

And 4. It assumes that we, as Methodist Preachers, are fully committed to its propagation.

That from the clear teaching of the Scriptures, the full and explicit statements of our doctrinal standards, as well as our own, well-understood covenant with the Church, and with God, when we were inducted into our holy office, there remains no doubt of the duty of spreading holiness, but simply arises a question, how best to perform the work, and reach so desirable an end.

Here, brothers, in a gospel of holiness, we poise ourselves, stand firmly, breathe freely, and rest sweetly in this green, yet sunny and healthful oasis, amid the fruitless deserts of doubt, and vacuity around.

The voices of truth, of the Church and of experience, blend in the divinest and sweetest symphony.

We assume, and I hope it is not a mere assumption, that wherever else the dove of holiness may fail to find rest for the sole of her foot, she is sure to find safety, and rest on the hand of the *faithful* Methodist preacher, outstretched from the bosom of the Church to welcome her.

The doctrine of Wesley and his compeers, of the fathers who planted Methodism in Western wilds, of all the greater and the lesser lights that have shone along the century of our toil and triumph as a Church, it is now, and we hope ever will be, the warmly cherished doctrine of their not unworthy successors.

And now, in regard to "methods" to be used, there are probably no *best* methods, as what may be the best method at one time and under given circumstances, may not be successful at another time and under other conditions. So, also, what may be the best method for one man may, in other hands, be a signal failure. Happily, we think, the Scriptures name no special methods, any more than special forms of ecclesiastical or civil government. And yet right methods are implied, and certainly not out of harmony with divine teaching. It may readily be conceded that any method which contravenes God's word, or that stirs the passions, or excites the curiosity without quickening the conscience, is illegitimate; or that ignores repentance, justification by faith, and such fundamental doctrines as taught by the Apostle, when "he reasoned of temperance, righteousness, and of a judgment to come," or that may not commend itself to the wisdom of the Church, and have in it the element of durability, at least adaptation to the wants of the average congregation, ought to be rejected. There are probably many innocent methods of arresting attention, awakening interest, and exciting a hunger for truth and righteousness among the people, in the use of which every pastor or minister, must be a law unto himself.

But whatever may or may not be adopted as aids or helps, God's methods are:

1. Clear personal experience. "Tarry ye at Jerusalem till

ye be endued with power from on high." Experience begets experience. No amount of theory, or eloquent presentation of the truth, without experience, will be as availing as with it. It is more encouraging to the people to say to them, "Come, let us go up at once and possess the land," or, "Come and hear all ye that fear God, and I will declare what He hath done for my soul." "As far as the east is from the west, so far hath he removed our transgressions from us."—Rather than to say to them, "The land is desirable, go ye up and gather the rich clusters of the ' grapes of Eshcol.' That which is good for our people is good for us."

In all our congregations are those who are sighing for full redemption, who are waiting to be led into the richer experiences of holiness. They tread lightly in the presence of their spiritual instructors, and eagerly watch the manifestation of the divine life and light in them. Encouraged by their example and approval, buds, blossoms, and fruits of grace, will mature in them, while, on the other hand, the chilling blasts of inexperience and indifference destroy all the buds of promise. As ministers, keeping the light-houses to guide souls over the treacherous sea of life, we cannot afford to let our own light burn dimly, or be obscured. To resist the tide of worldliness, sinful amusements, business pressure, and general spiritual atrophy, our people need the inspiration of personal experience in the pastor.

2. We name, definite, full, and frequent preaching of holiness, as an essential method of spreading it. The frequency of its presentation in the pulpit should be regulated by its relative importance in the catalogue of Bible doctrines.

If it be the central truth of Christianity, if in its sweep it so bears upon all the great interests of Christ's Church, as that they wither and die when it is omitted, if by its neglect, the life-blood of the Church moves slowly, avarice and greed grow apace, conscience becomes dull, finances are a burden, and collections go a begging, and spiritual declension becomes a crushing burden on the heart of the minister; is it *wise* to relegate this doctrine to the obscurest time and place in our pulpit work?  It is certainly very unseemly for a minister to be forward in presenting his own fancied originality, far-fetched speculations, crude philosophies, and unscientific vagaries, to be ever shaking Huxley's dry bones before us, or be orating on juiceless evolutionism, as though *these* were the alpha and omega of a minister's work; rather, than presenting us the great things of the law, judgment, mercy, and truth, and especially that holiness without which no man shall see the Lord.  We would by no means encourage "one ideaism."  But it is manifestly better to have one absorbing *gospel* IDEA, than to have no idea at all, especially that can give nourishment to the hungry soul.

There are men I presume so afraid of riding a hobby, as to go to the other extreme of never preaching this doctrine at all.  Surely of all the hobbies men employ to ride into notoriety, or obtain a following, this were the least dangerous.

We should not be slow to excuse a man who feels that the zeal of the Lord hath eaten him up, or that the flame of holiness is like the Prophet's fire shut up in his bones, who in his eager pursuit of souls, *seems* to make a hobby of this theme, which is to him more than the philosopher's stone, or than "Aladdin's lamp."

Good strong common sense will usually be a sufficient safeguard in this matter.  There are times for preaching the law, and pursuing the sinner with its flashing penalties, for opening the horrors of the damned, or, on the other hand expatiating on the beauties of heaven, or eulogizing the ethics and moralities of Christianity, but in all, and over all, with the Apostle, "this one thing we do," seek to spread scriptural holiness.

3. Another method of importance is the press.  Tracts,

periodicals, and books must be sent as swift-winged messengers with the glad tidings. No great movement can succeed in this age without the press. Let this stream of salvation flow pure and clear into the literature of the Church, with its multiplied agencies for permeating the whole land, and its power must be felt in giving tone to piety, grace and solidity to character, and beauty and strength to the Church.

To what degree efforts should be made outside of the regularly appointed channels of publication, or official publishing interest of the Church, is probably an open question. In loyalty to the Church I yield to no man, but if it should come to pass, which I cannot say ever has been the case, that official organs fail to give due prominence to this subject, or Agents or Editors will not publish in its interest, then I know of no other or better remedy than outside publications. We cheerfully admit the necessity and benefit of one or two monthlies, or weekly periodicals, making a specialty of holiness and experience. But it does seem to me a great misfortune to fritter away our strength in originating outside publications, whose name is legion; many of the feeble, sickly bantlings, which have no claim upon us only that of sympathy, to save them from a premature decay and death, which might in some way bring a degree of reproach upon the blessed doctrine we seek to advance. And yet I would not be arbitrary or contentious, but entertain the broadest charity towards those who differ with me in view. But in all candor, it seems to me we shall be able better to serve the cause of Christ, and spread holiness, by using the agencies we have more vigorously, rather than by starting new enterprises, and distracting the attention of the Church by the multitude of new agencies, the unintentional working of which may be to tear down and destroy. Better by far, we think, to turn the many little streams into one mighty river, strong to overcome and sweep away obstructions. But bating all these things, we reiterate the statement before made, that the use of the press is a method of so much power, that it must never be left unemployed.

4. As a "method," special meetings for the promotion of holiness have been much employed, and I presume will claim attention in this discussion.

Upon this subject, there are of course, various views. On the one hand it is said, "all our religious services are for the promotion of holiness," and it would sound strange to call a meeting for "the promotion of justification by faith, or the witness of the Spirit, or any one of the special doctrines of our holy religion." And yet the only objection to this kind of a call may be our unfamiliarity with it. And, is it not true, that we have special meetings for all other questions, temperance, Sunday-school, class-meetings, and all moral reforms? Why then may not believers meet for this special work? There is directness of object, unity of aim and feeling, heartiness of devotion, and strength of desire, as well as freedom from the restraints of a promiscuous assembly, which are evidently greatly in favor of these special meetings.

They keep the subject in mind, compel closer self-examination, and give us the benefit of the deepest experiences of the Church. All this probably can be had in well-attended class-meetings, where the theme of holiness is pre eminently absorbing. But brethren, there is no danger that our people will become too holy or too enthusiastic in Christ's cause. Instead of opposing these meetings, directly or indirectly, would it not be a wiser and better thing, to go into them, control and encourage them, and profit by them and by all other outcroppings of religious fervor among the people, and thus prevent the possibility of their misuse, in the development of fanaticism on the one hand, or sour godliness on the other. As in business life, men succeed who employ all right means, overcome obstacles, overlook the follies of others, brook many irregularities, and fret not because of evil doers, but press straight for the mark in view, so we must be "instant in season, and out of season," employ regular or irregular means, overlook many things not as we would have them, but by all honorable means, save souls if possible. What do we, or should we care for methods, so they are not sinful; it is *results* we seek. The spirit of Methodism, as well as the liberty of the gospel bursts all fetters, and rejects all methods however ancient and approved, that stand in the way of the salvation of souls.

And now a word in regard to "the proprieties to be regarded" in this work. I suppose this means we should have due regard for each other's rights, that we should "consider one another, to provoke unto love and to good works." That we should *avoid* all assumption of superior piety, or appearance of discourtesy to those who may not agree with our views. That as friends and advocates of holiness, we should never belittle ourselves, by disparaging others, especially our preacher by speaking of him, or praying for him in public, as though he, either backslid or unconverted, were an enemy to holiness, because he forsooth may not speak our shibboleth.

Little improprieties may greatly hinder the work. To be always harping upon a dead church, to speak of the official members of the church as opposed to this doctrine, and in various ways in the pulpit and out of it, to make the impression on the outside world, that all have bowed the knee to Baal, and that we alone are left to defend this doctrine, and championize the truth, is to say the least unfortunate. If we cannot do anything for the truth, let us not do anything against it. The amenities of Christian life, and the proprieties to be regarded, are doubtless tersely and beautifully expressed by the Apostle Paul, in the uses and limitations of that focal centre of Gospel truth and light, called " CHARITY."

We shall not go wide of the mark, if we are guided by that wisdom which is from above, which is pure, peaceable, easy to be entreated, full of mercy and good fruits, without partiality and without hypocrisy." Let us exalt Christ, hold up the Cross, preach, and live holiness, receive and enjoy the baptism of the Holy Ghost, as we go forth to spread holiness over the land.

By vote, Brother Ketcham was respectfully requested to furnish his article for publication, with the others which have been read.

Benediction by Brother Weeks.

---

*Evening.*

After prayer by Bro. Krehbiel, an interesting address "On the progress of the work of full salvation among the Germans in Europe and America," was delivered by Dr. Nast ; a vote of thanks was tendered him.

The Committee on Unity of Operations in the various holiness organizations reported :

Your Committee to whom was referred the subject of " Combining in some way in harmonious action the various organizations interested in the holiness movement " respectfully submit the following recommendation, and ask to be excused from making farther report at this time, but to have the privilege of farther considering the subject among themselves by correspondence hereafter, and of reporting .their conclusions, should any be reached, through the press :

*Resolved,* That the Secretaries of the various associations interested in the holiness movement be requested, not later than the fifteenth day of October of each year, to forward to the Secretary of the National Association at Philadelphia and to the Secretary of each other organization, a succinct statement of the work of his association for the year past, and, as nearly as can be ascertained of its plans for the succeeding year; that their various reports, in condensed form, be published in the various holiness papers for the information and encouragement of all interested in the work.

Respectfully submitted.

W. T. PERKINS, *Chairman.*

Adopted.

Editors to whom the papers presented were referred for publication were authorized to so abbreviate them as to prevent undue bulkiness in the volume.

Thanks were tendered the Trustees, Pastor, and friends in Wesley Chapel, for the use of their house and their kindness.

The Secretary was authorized to write up the Minutes through to-morrow evening, December 2d, and the Conference adjourned, *sine die.*

---

*Fifth Day.*

All the exercises of the Sabbath, December 2d, will be devotional; a Love Feast was held from nine o'clock to eleven, A. M., in which all who testified, and they were many, witnessed to the power of the blood to save now from all sin.

At eleven o'clock, Bro. J. S. Inskip preached from Rev. 12: 10–12, formulating it by saying that the present intensity of evil among men is destined to a speedy and complete overthrow by the blood of the Lamb and the *word* of testimony, the atonement and confirmatory experience.

At three o'clock, P. M., Bro. J. P. Brooks preached from Gal. 5: 11. Subject: The offence of the cross.

At half-past seven o'clock, P. M., Bro. Wm. McDonald preached from Acts 6: 8, a sermon attended by the sanction of the Holy Ghost.

Altar exercises followed each of these sermons with blessed and saving results.

The Conference has been one of increasing spirituality, the souls of the brethren entering into sweeter fellowship in Jesus.

Adjourned, *sine die*, with the benediction.

W. T. PERKINS, } *Secretaries.*
S. WEEKS,

# HOLINESS CONFERENCE.

———

NEW YORK, *December 11th*, 1877.

The plan of holding Conventions for the Promotion of Holiness is eminently wise. At the recent one in New York city, the precious results were manifest at every session. Many will forever praise God for those days of power. The essays embraced various topics of vital interest bearing upon the main subject, the sermons were aflame with the fire of the Holy Ghost, and the consecration and prayer meetings were seasons of pentecostal power. Both the interest and the attendance increased daily, and culminated on the Sabbath in an overwhelming baptism of the Spirit.

The Convention was opened on Tuesday evening, 11th, with a consecration meeting, and was formally organized on Wednesday, A. M., the 12th, by the election of Bro. Inskip as President, Bro. B. M. Adams, Vice-President, I. Simmons and W. P. Smith, Secretaries. Subsequently Bro. Wm. F. Ladd, of the Friends, and Dr. Ball, of the Presbyterian Church, were elected as Vice-Presidents.

Following the organization, reports were heard from the Churches. Dr. L. R. Dunn gave an encouraging account of the progress of holiness in Halsey St., Newark. I. Simmons spoke for Fleet St., Brooklyn, Bro. Adams for Central Church, and Bro. J. Parker for South Second St. Sister Amanda Smith, at present laboring on Staten Island, gave an inspiring report of the work. Others represented various Churches and holiness meetings, from all which we conclude that holiness, as a distinct blessing, is rapidly spreading through the Church, and that the day has past for either authorities or unbelief to put preventing hands upon it.

The afternoon session was preceded by a powerful prayer-meeting, led by Bro. John Parker. At the appointed hour, Dr. Dunn read an interesting essay on "The relation of Methodist ministers to the doctrine of holiness." Following the reading was an instructive discussion of the main subject. Would God that our thousands of ministers were living in the clear enjoyment of perfect love, and with red-hot periods were preaching it to their congregations!

In the evening, Bro. J. E. Searles read an excellent essay on "The history of the present revival of holiness."

## A BRIEF SKETCH OF THE HOLINESS REVIVAL; ESPECIALLY OF THE ORIGIN AND WORK OF "THE NATIONAL CAMP MEETING ASSOCIATION FOR THE PROMOTION OF HOLINESS."

REV. J. E. SEARLES.

The doctrine of justification by faith distinguished the teaching of Martin Luther, and was the clear-ringing key-note of the Reformation. But the doctrine of "Christian perfection" was promulgated at a more recent date. Though George Fox, the founder of the society called Friends, taught that it was the privilege of Christians to be fully saved from sin, and was imprisoned, and greatly persecuted for professing full salvation nearly a hundred years before the Wesleys raised the banner of holiness; yet they and their co-adjutors were the real evangelists of this higher form of Christian doctrine and experience.

More than anything else definite, this was their theme in preaching, and the raising up of holy people was the result at which they aimed in their ministry.

Mr. Wesley says : " My brother and I read the Bible, saw inward and outward holiness therein, followed after it, and invited others to do so. He saw that holiness comes by faith, and that we must be justified before we are sanctified ; but holiness was our point, inward and outward holiness. God then thrust us out to raise up a people. This (he says) was the rise of Methodism."

This doctrine and experience was preached and urged upon believers, also by the founders of the Methodist Church in this country. And perfect love, or sanctification, was a common experience in the Church, and a large proportion of the ministers professed the experience.

In the days of Bishops Asbury and Whatcoat, both of whom professed full salvation, hundreds were sometimes converted at quarterly meetings, and at the camp meetings held in those days, it is recorded that as many as eleven hundred were converted, and six hundred sanctified at one Camp Meeting ; and at another the astonishing number, of thirteen hundred, were converted and nine hundred sanctified. And they always, as a general thing, held their Camp Meetings over Sunday, and Sunday was the day of the mightiest victories.

But about the middle of the century preaching on the subject became more formal, and the experience as a consequence waned, and the love of many waxed cold.

Some thirty years ago, however, there was a revival of the doctrine and experience, especially in western New York which, by reason of opposition and persecution, resulted in the " Nazarite " movement, and ultimately in the " Free Methodist " organization.

Co-incident with this movement in the West, the doctrine

and experience were revived in the city of New York. Mrs. Phebe Palmer, the Hester Ann Rogers of American Methodism, was raised up as a teacher and writer on the subject of holiness.

She and her husband, Dr. Palmer, opened their house for special meetings for the promotion of this higher experience, and for nearly forty years this special service has been held every Tuesday afternoon of each week. During these years persons from almost every Christian land have visited this holiness meeting; and multitudes have been instructed and led into the King's highway of perfect love.

Mrs. Palmer and her husband have traveled extensively in Canada, in Europe, as well as in this country, teaching and preaching the full freedom of the soul from sin through faith in the blood of Christ. The judgment day only will fully reveal their marvelous success in bringing sinners to Christ, and believers to the fountain of cleansing.

I might mention many others, cotemporaneous with Mrs. Palmer—as for instance Bishop Hamline, of precious memory; Dr. N. Bangs, and Rev. James Caughey.

But it is expected in this brief sketch that I shall give some facts that may be of interest respecting the origin and work of " The National Camp Meeting Association for the Promotion of Holiness."

We think it will appear quite evident to all unbiased minds that The National Camp Meeting Association had a providential origin in a Camp Meeting held at Vineland, N. J., July 17, 1867;—the special object of which was the promotion of Christian holiness.

The fact that many ministers and members of the Church have not been able to see the propriety and importance of this revival agency, is to our mind the clearest evidence of its necessity.

The origin of the Association was on this wise:—Rev.

Wm. B. Osborn, a member of the New Jersey Conference, had experienced the blessing of full salvation, and under its inspiration, he, together with the Brothers Stockton, preached the doctrine and experience pretty generally throughout the lower section of the State ; and a very considerable interest was awakened on the subject in the Churches.

In his thinking how the work might be extended, it was suggested to his mind that a *Camp Meeting* might be held for this special object.

Under the impulse of this grand idea he came to New York, and laid the suggestion before Rev. Mr. Inskip, then pastor of the Green Street M. E. Church, who also had come into the same experience. Mr. Inskip was deeply moved and impressed that the suggestion was of the Lord.

After discussing the subject, and praying earnestly that they might know the mind of the Spirit, all doubt vanished from their minds, and they joined hands resolving, Providence permitting, such a Camp Meeting should be held at some suitable place, and there should be at least *two tents* on the grounds.

After consulting with judicious and reliable friends of the cause, it was determined to issue a public call for a meeting of ministers and laymen who were in sympathy with the movement to make arrangements for the proposed meeting. This call was signed by Rev. A. E. Ballard, P. E. N. J. Conference, Revs. H. M. Brown, R. V. Lawrence, W. B. Osborn, J. A. Wood, B. M. Adams, G. C. M. Roberts, of Baltimore, A. K. Street, G. Hughes, J. S. Heisler, J. S. Inskip, A. Longacre, and A. Cookman.

Pursuant to this call, the meeting convened at Philadelphia June 13, 1867, to authorize and arrange for the *first* Camp Meeting ever held for the specific and special purpose of promoting the work of entire sanctification. This meeting was largely attended by the most distinguished ministers and laymen in the Church; and it is worthy of note they were all of one mind and heart.

The Resolution to hold the meeting was offered by Rev. A. Atwood, in the following terms: " *Resolved*, That we hold a Camp Meeting for the specific work of promoting heart purity." The resolution passed *unanimously*. Now who can object to *such a work ?* Or who can object to *the means chosen* to promote it?

It was also Resolved on the same occasion, that this Camp Meeting should be named, "The National Camp Meeting for the promotion of Holiness."

This in brief is the history of the origin of this association, heard of, and known to some extent in every Christian land.

And this movement thus inaugurated for the promotion of the higher Christian life, has become a fact, and is constituting at the present day an important part of the history of the Christian church.

Space will only allow us to say, this First National Camp Meeting for the promotion of holiness, was wonderful in its character and results; exceeding by far all the highest anticipations of its originators.

Never perhaps since the day of Pentecost was there more signal manifestations of the Spirit and power of God to purify human hearts and save sinners.

And at the close of the meeting the great congregation of devout worshipers, requested by a unanimous rising vote that another meeting for the same object be held the next year.

After the vote of the people it was judged expedient to form a permanent association. And the preachers who had conducted the meeting gathered in a tent and kneeling in a circle, made the organization, appointed officers, and completed the whole arrangement on their knees. And none of that company will ever forget the prayer of the sainted Cookman on the occasion; the silent power of the spirit world came upon all hearts, and all were overwhelmingly conscious of the presence and indwelling of the Holy Spirit; the face of each shone with a heavenly radiance and perfect love was enthroned in each heart.

While this was the practical commencement, the original cause of this great movement lay back of these official and formal acts. It is a deeply interesting fact that for some time antecedent to the organization of these special camp meeting services, those who were specially interested in the cause of holiness among all denominations had been praying that some way might be provided and some efficient means employed by which the doctrine and experience of Christian purity might be more generally taught and more thoroughly and clearly set before the people. This great holiness movement throughout the land therefore is God's practical answer to the prayers of His saints.

And as a denominational expedient, this organized movement was considered highly important by some of the wisest and best men in the Church, not only for the aid and comfort of those who profess the experience of perfect love, or might be seeking after it; but especially to save this only distinguishing doctrine of Methodism from becoming obsolete; which was, and still is, opposed and ridiculed by many ministers, and as a consequence by many of the laity.

In view, therefore, of these and other considerations relative to this effort to maintain the original teaching of the Church on this subject, and its original design to spread scripture holiness over these lands, we may rest assured that this is at least a part of God's plan to bring the Church back to her former simplicity and purity; that she may thus be endowed with moral power to accomplish her high mission.

The Association from the beginning has had no systematic rules, or written code of laws for its government, but has in all cases sought to be under the guidance of the Holy Spirit in all their plans and efforts.

A President, Vice President, and Secretary have constituted the officers. In a few instances a temporary Treasurer has been appointed. But most of their financial transactions have been, the payment of considerable sums out of their pockets.

The number of members has on an average been about twenty. Some have passed on to their glorious reward ; a few have retired from *active* co-operation with the Association. And if some have weakened a little, none have, so far as we know, backslidden from the faith.

But notwithstanding these losses, the Lord has raised up others to fill their places, so that now the Association is larger than at any former period, and never perhaps, was sustained by a corps of more able and effective laborers.

Great responsibility as a matter of course has rested upon the President, who in the nature of the case would be looked to as the Leader in this great work.

The manner in which the work has been carried forward has required a Leader of almost superhuman endurance, as well as of marked ability :—a man of tact and skill to manage the multitude, and comprehend the situation at a glance. In the good providence of God we think such a man has filled the place from the beginning.

And it is also a matter of gratulation that he has been seconded, encouraged, and aided by the efficient co-operation, the calm and steady movement of the Vice President; and thus a happy balance of effectiveness has always been maintained by the contact of two extremes !

And it is clear to all unbiased minds, that the mantle of the fathers whose spiritual enthusiasm stirred the stagnant elements of religious society in two continents, has fallen upon the men of this work.

And just at this point I may add,—the teachings of this association are nothing *new* or *strange :*—This teaching is

6

nothing less or more than that of the standard authors of the Church, Wesley, Fletcher, Watson, Clarke, Asbury, Hedding, Bangs, Olin, Fisk, Hamline, Foster, Peck and scores of others that might be mentioned, living and dead; all of whom recognized and taught entire sanctification, or Christian perfection as the distinguishing doctrine of Methodism.

And though good and learned men may not entirely coincide with Mr. Wesley and these authorities or they may conceive of the attainment of the same experience by other approaches; it will be seen that the National Association in making a "*specialty*" of preaching holiness at their Camp Meetings, and urging it upon believers, have in an intensified form followed the instructions and example of Mr. Wesley and the early preachers of Methodism.

And it will also be observed that the teaching of the Association is corroborated by the experience of men and women whose names distinguish the history of Methodism both in Europe and in this country, who have testified clearly and unhesitatingly to the instantaneous cleansing of their hearts from all sin by faith in the blood of Christ.

What, therefore, is the logical sequence of these facts? Does it not plainly appear that the National Association for the promotion of holiness in their work, of all others, not excepting the Bishops, are especially loyal to Methodism and the Church?

This Association is seeking only to glorify God in building up the Church in holiness, and bringing sinners to repentance and salvation. And yet, notwithstanding their work is thus open and apparent to all, a technical ecclesiasticism is somewhat nettled, because this movement is a "specialty, self-appointed, and schismatical."

This criticism might be retorted: What is there in the Methodist Church besides preaching the gospel, and the two Sacraments, that is not a "specialty?"

And we might add the titles of dignity worn with so much grace by many, are a "specialty," scarcely warranted by the word of God. And it will also be seen by the thoughtful and more intelligent, that the doctrine of entire sanctification, is the only doctrine that gives us any reasonable or consistent ground at all *for our existence as a Church :* all the other doctrines we hold, were in the Mother Church : this *one only* is a strictly Methodist doctrine.

Our Bishops urge greater liberality in the contributions for missionary work, but seem to overlook what one sanctified minister did in India, independent of missionary funds and of all ecclesiastical machinery.

It really ought to be perceived by the leaders of our Zion that this higher form of Christian doctrine and experience, which is *the* spiritual stand-point of our Church, is an advanced step towards the more speedy conversion of the world.

It appears to us therefore, that it should be a matter of thanksgiving that a movement has been organized to make the teaching of this doctrine more specific and prominent; especially as it had so faded from the recognition of the Church that many ministers as well as members regarded it as a cast-off garment fit only to be hung up in some old ecclesiastical garret !

It is exceedingly comforting to the Association, and they do give thanks to the great Head of the Church, that in every place He has set His seal of approbation and blessing upon their humble endeavors.

The Association has held thirty-four National Camp Meetings, distributed through at least fifteen different States of the Union ; besides Tabernacle Meetings held on both shores of the continent. All these meetings have been of the most intensely spiritual character, as all can testify who remember Vineland, Manheim, Oakington, Des Plains, Round Lake, Hamilton, Urbana, Cedar Rapids, and every other place where these meetings have been held, has been a scene of pentecostal power and baptism of the Holy Spirit.

Thousands of ministers and multitudes of members of the Churches have attended these meetings, and have been quickened in their religious experience and life, and great numbers of the clergy and laity have come into the enjoyment of full salvation, and thousands of sinners have also been converted. Many of our greatest preachers have become advocates of the cause, and are flaming heralds of this special doctrine of Methodism. Also, many periodicals in the interest of the "Higher life" experience have been published; and Holiness Associations have been organized in many parts of the country, and State organizations for the purpose of holding camp-meetings to promote the cause of holiness.

This Holiness revival has also given the temperance cause an impulse that it never had before; and laborers have gone forth in the might of an all-conquering faith, endowed with a moral power before which the rum traffic of the land has stood appalled! And it is only by this sign of the Cross in the Higher life that the temperance army can conquer, and achieve a final triumph.

It is likewise clear to those who are conversant with all the facts connected with this work, that every vital interest of the Church has been promoted by the labors of this association. Thousands of books published by the "Methodist Book Concern" have been sold and circulated through this medium. And large sums of money have been contributed to benevolent objects in the Church as the result of this movement. How could it be otherwise than that the Church should be benefited, when their teachings require that all consecrate themselves and all they have to God to be used for His glory?

It is indeed evident to any one who has made himself acquainted with this great movement, that the whole Christian Church has felt more or less the life-giving impulse on both continents, and in a clearly defined consciousness has got a list in the direction of a higher spirituality.

It is a pleasant coincidence that this National Association dates its origin from the memorable centenary of American Methodism. And from its standpoint of holiness and entire consecration it would seem that the Lord raised up this agency to give the Church a new spiritual send-off as she enters upon her work of the next hundred years. And we think it is not egotistic to say, the religion of the whole American Protestant Church has not only been energized by this great revival of the higher life idea, but its mission is also to reflect an irresistible influence upon the Protestant formalism of other countries.

If this be the fact, how fearful is the responsibility of some in their endeavor to hinder it ! *God knows* that we nor any body else are likely to be any *too good*, at the best. No effort, therefore, is needed to lower the tone of piety in the Church.

As the work of the Association is more generally known in the Eastern States, I may note with a little more particularity the result of their visit and labors on the Pacific coast and at Salt Lake City. This I may do, as I am under unspeakable obligations to the brethren for the benefit I received on that occasion.

The Association had received frequent and pressing invitations from influential ministers and members of the Church in California to hold a series of Tabernacle services in that State for the promotion of Christian holiness. And the low spiritual condition of the Church was urged as a reason for the holding such services.

It is difficult for a stranger to conceive of the real facts in the case. Experimental religion, with some honorable exceptions, was ignored, and wickedness and worldliness seemed to have full sway.

It no doubt seemed like an absurdity to many good people

that the brethren of the Association should go 3,000 miles to hold special services for the promotion of holiness under such circumstances. It would naturally be said, you had better *"get the Church to work, and get sinners converted."* But to those who are acquainted with the work, it is clear that this holiness movement was the only thing that could reach the case.

The unconverted were well used to the old methods of getting up revivals, and had lost all confidence in them, and paid no regard to them whatever. A minister could go into a bar-room, or saloon, and preach and pray all he pleased, and the people would listen; and after the service was ended, the drinking and card-playing would be resumed, as though nothing of the kind had transpired.

But when these men heard *professors and backsliders* called to account for their unfaithfulness and neglect of duty, and want of fidelity to Christian principle, and were required to confess and repent, and come out from the world and consecrate themselves to God, they said, "This is the true kind of preaching; these men go down to bed rock." And, as might be expected, when they came in for their share of the preaching, they were stricken with conviction, and sought the Lord by scores and hundreds. Thus it was abundantly manifest that this mission of the brethren, and their special method to promote holiness, was signally blessed of the Lord, and made a means of a Pentecostal outpouring of the Spirit such as never before had been experienced by the Church in the Golden State.

These Tabernacle meetings from eight to ten days each were held respectively in *Sacramento, Santa Clara,* and *San Francisco.*

The meetings at all these places were, indeed, occasions of marvelous spiritual manifestations. Time will not permit of any detailed account. But we have no recollection of ever hear-

ing in the same space of time so many sermons of such simplicity and power, searching the hearts of saint and sinner.
The word of the Lord swept through the ranks of the gathered
thousands like a tempest of fire, overthrowing every refuge of
lies, leaving all standing at the judgment seat of a quickened
conscience and of the word of God. Satan raged, and hell
beat to arms; but the "Lion of Judah" gave them the victory
again and again; some cases of conversion seemed quite mirac-
ulous, and cases of sanctification were equally overwhelming
and wonderful—*my own* among the rest.

During some periods of the meetings presiding elders, pastors and other ministers were stricken to the ground by the
power of God, and lay for hours entirely powerless, but
filled with glory !

As a result of these meetings, as near as we could estimate,
from 300 to 400 professed conversion, and nearly double
that number were sanctified; including the leading ministers
and members of the Church.

A correspondent of the California *Christian Advocate* wrote
as follows :

" Never in the history of California has so remarkable a
meeting been held. Never have we seen such displays of divine power in the awakening and conversion of sinners. Men
and women who have not been in church for twelve or fifteen
years have found the pearl of great price. Slaves to rum and
opium, and tobacco, have been thoroughly saved, though the
chains had been on them for eighteen years. Men of afflu-
ence have found their way to the cross."

At the close of the Santa Clara meeting, the following pre-
amble and resolutions were read before a congregation of some
three or four thousand people—to wit :

" The undersigned ministers of the M. E. Church in attendance on the Tabernacle Services, at the Santa Clara Camp
meeting, California Conference, May 1871, take this method

of expressing their thanksgiving to God, and their appreciation of the labor of the National Committee for the promotion of Christian Holiness, consisting of Rev. Messrs. Inskip, McDonald, Boole, Coleman, Osborn and Searles. (The brethren had voted me a member, pro tem., of the committee; and on their return I was confirmed as a member by the annual meeting.) It is therefore

*Resolved*, That we have rejoiced in the wonderful outpouring of the Holy Spirit, witnessed in connection with the labors of our eastern brethren at this place; and that we recognize in them the unction which rested on our fathers, and acknowledge the seal of divine approval on the ministry of these evangelists.

*Resolved*, That we pledge our united prayers and labors for the continuance of the spiritual revival begun under such favorable auspices.

*Resolved*, That our prayers and cordial sympathy will accompany our brethren in their subsequent efforts, particularly on the Pacific slope, and in Utah.

J. W. Ross, P. E., San Francisco District.

W. J. McClay, Pastor, San Jose.

J. H. Wythe, Pastor, Santa Clara.

D. A. Dryden, Pastor, Gilroy.

C. H. Aflerbach, Pastor, German Church, San Jose.

A. B. Brueck, " " " " Francisco.

A. Copland, " Monterey.

C. A. Hertel, " Antioch.

C. O. Belknap, " Dixon.

J. Daniel, Supt. Minister.

T. H. Sinex, President University of the Pacific.

H. C. Benson, Editor California *Christian Advocate*.

A. J. Nelson, Professor University of the Pacific.

A. K. Crawford, " " " "

E. A. Hazen, P. E., Marysville District.

The San Francisco meeting was the greatest. The work there was amazing. The most wealthy and influential members of the Churches entered into the experience of full salvation. The preachers were hearty in their co-operation, as well as the Presiding Elder, and the brethren at the Book Room, all of whom were in the fullest sympathy with the work. Brethren from distant charges came in large numbers, and returned to their fields of labor filled with the Spirit. And all united in the statement that this was the most wonderful meeting ever held on the Pacific coast. Never had San Francisco been so deeply moved before by any religious interest.

Dr. Benson said, in his notice of the meeting, in the California *Christian Advocate* :

"A hallowed influence pervaded the congregations. The Spirit and unction of the Holy One rested on the worshiping people. Large numbers were brought into the light and liberty of the Gospel in its rich and abounding fullness. Many souls made a profession of faith in Christ. There were those present and participating in the exercises who were communicants of other Churches. All seemed to be filled with the same spirit, and to speak the same language. We have never witnessed more signal displays of divine power. There was zeal, but according to knowledge ; there was enthusiasm, yet it was free from uncurbed excitement. All felt that the Master of assemblies was present."

Thousands, it was said, the last evening were unable to gain admittance into the Tabernacle. The meeting was a great triumph for the cause of holiness.

The visit of the Association to Salt Lake City, was of more importance than can be appreciated by persons not acquainted with the civil and religious condition of society there. The Methodist Church had established a mission in the city, and had purchased a lot for the erection of a Church at some future date. It was hoped that the Tabernacle meeting might awaken a new interest in their behalf throughout the country; which it did.

Bro. G. M. Pierce, the Missionary, exerted himself, and left nothing undone that was in his power to make the meeting a success. But so restricted was free speech, and so absolute the intolerance of Mormon superstition, many had but little hope that we would be permitted to hold the meeting, if indeed, we all escaped with our lives. Those who knew most about the state of things, acknowledged that it required no little pluck to pitch our Tabernacle in the very heart of the great metropolis of Mormondom, and hold a series of public meetings for the purpose, in fact, of exposing their whole religious system as an unmitigated fraud and imposition upon the credulity of mankind.

But, *the meeting was held according to appointment.*

The number of conversions was not perhaps as large as might have been expected, but we had no just reasons under the circumstances to have expected more. The real work of the occasion was to sow seed for future harvest. But the meeting was not without immediate fruits.

Among those converted was the wife of Bishop Hunter, called the archbishop of Mormonism. She was gloriously converted, and resolved to assume her maiden name and wash her hands completely of Mormonism. The wife and daughter of Orson Pratt, the ablest advocate of the Mormon faith, were among those who embraced religion. The first wife of Godbie, the leader of the Godbieites, was also among the seekers, and abandoned polygamy. Others long under the heel of Mormon despotism, and those not Mormons were converted or reclaimed, and some of the very few professors of religion in the city entered into the enjoyment of full salvation. The salvation of these few souls in Salt Lake City at the time, was a greater achievement than the conversion of Lydia, and the casting the evil spirit out of the damsel at Philippi.

It must be remembered that Brigham and his high officials attended the Tabernacle services, overawing the people with their presence; and all who gave any countenance or support to the meetings were sure to become the subjects of persecution, if not of secret vengeance. It was therefore akin to embracing martyrdom to apostatize from Mormonism.

But second only to the salvation of souls and the salutary impulse given to the cause of true religion, the grand result of this meeting was the triumphant vindication of *the right of free speech*, in a city where many had paid the forfeiture of their lives for claiming the same right.

During the meetings the most searching truths were boldly proclaimed, truths which struck at the very foundation of the great Mormon imposition.

United States officials and army officers present, were highly gratified with the efforts and results of the meeting. They declared that the meeting had done more to lift the people up from a state of slavish repression and cowardice to actual personal self-assertion and freedom, than anything that had ever transpired before in Utah.

This was plainly manifest in the fact that, while Brigham Young, *being present*, was denounced as a man who had outraged the laws of Christian civilization, and under the garb of religion had set aside the law of God by multiplying the number of his wives, and had perpetrated the foulest iniquity! And while others of his officials present were charged with the most revolting wrongs and cruelties, and with having hands stained with the blood of their innocent victims, whose ghosts haunted the canons of their mountains and walked their streets at midnight, hundreds of people applauded by clapping their hands! But *those* men responded *only* by their pale faces and their silence!

Thousands of people, mostly Mormons (of course), attended the meeting, and many from twelve and fifteen miles out of the city, driving in with mule teams, in wagons loaded with two and three wives and their children. And, what is an interesting fact, a large number of these people never heard a gospel sermon before. They knew only Mormonism—they never heard any thing else.

Mormonism received a blow from that Tabernacle meeting from which it never has recovered, and never will.

That meeting also accomplished the masterly result of putting Mormonism *on the defensive.* This fact was clearly brought out in a letter written by Rev. Mr. Talmage, and published in *The Christian at Work.* Mr. Talmage visited Salt Lake City some time subsequent to the Tabernacle meeting. He says: "We found the track of the Methodist tent all the way across the Continent. Mormonism never received such a shot as when, with Brigham Young and his elders present in the tent, the party of wide-awake Methodist ministers preached righteousness, temperance, and judgment to come in great Salt Lake City. The effect of those few days of faithful talking will never be forgotten. Hardly a service is held in the Mormon Tabernacle that an effort is not made to combat the sermons of the *Itinerants.* On the two occasions I was present in the Tabernacle, all the speakers felt called upon to answer the Big Tent. It was evident that the monster of sin had been speared, and the wound rankled." And he adds: "We have never seen the brethren of that religious storming party—but we hail them through these columns for the glorious work they have accomplished in Salt Lake City."

But I must not dwell longer on the details of this work.

The Association, by special invitation, are to hold several camp-meetings the ensuing season : and it is also a matter of interest that the State Association already formed, and others about to be organized will grandly supply the service, which it is impossible for the " National " to render.

And individual Churches in almost every part of the country are holding weekly meetings for the promotion of this work. By all these means the cause is being strengthened, and the work is spreading, and the cloud of witnesses is accumulating stretching out over all lands, and to the remoter missions in heathen climes.

Dr. J. P. Newman became convinced of his need of this great experience, by conversing with a Presbyterian Missionary in China, who enjoyed the blessing of full salvation.

"Thanks be to God who giveth us the victory through our Lord Jesus Christ."

In conclusion, allow me to refer to our publishing interest. In connection with our Camp Meeting Association, we have organized an association called "*The National Publishing Association for the Promotion of Holiness*." This is separate from the other, but somewhat under its auspicies.

This Association owns an establishment in the city of Philadelphia, on one of the principal streets, affording ample accommodations for their work now, also when it shall become indefinitely extended.

In addition to two periodicals published—a weekly paper, "The Christian Standard and Home Journal," edited by Rev. Mr. Inskip, and the "Advocate of Holiness," a monthly, edited by Rev. Mr. McDonald,—we have a depository of the best books, tracts, and music, on the subject of the higher Christian life, to be found in the world. And the Association is scattering them broad-cast over the earth. Our periodicals and books go into India, China, Germany, England, Ireland, Scotland, and all Europe.

This publishing interest may appear to some a little on the line of opposition, or at least to some unnecessary. But those who are at all conversant with the subject must see, especially from our stand-point the great utility of it. We think it manifestly a *necessity*, that the Association should **have some means** of communicating with the Church at large, in all Christian countries; for our work is world-wide, and extends beyond the bounds of any one Church organ.

And then it is highly important that the Association have the means to publish their statement of doctrine and experience on the subject of full salvation, as well as books and tracts on the same line; which they could not reasonably expect to have published to the extent desirable and as needed, in the regular Church papers.

And from various circumstances it was clearly manifest that if they were allowed the use of such periodicals, our publications would elicit controversy, and thus stir up strife in the Church, and be a means of evil, and not of good; for some are ready even to antagonize and controvert this only distinctive doctrine of their own Church. Strife in the Church, is the farthest from the desire or intention of these servants of Christ. Wisdom, therefore, and Christian prudence dictated the course pursued.

And surely all good people should rejoice to see agencies multiplied for furnishing such literature as tends to encourage men and women to live holy lives, consecrated to God. And by God's blessing we expect the pious traveller will read our imprint in books and periodicals in every nation under the whole heavens, where the sign of the cross is displayed. Thus by the Press and the active agency of the Association in holding *Camp Meetings, Tabernacle, and other meetings,* they hope to extend the work in the Church, and also through these instrumentalities to raise up and set in operation other agencies; many of which have already appeared in a variety of periodicals, books, and organizations for the promotion of this higher experience in believers.

Finally—the circumstances of the times are calling to us to re-double our efforts and press this battle of the Lord! Intemperance stalks abroad,—vice and immorality fester in high places as well as in low; infidelity and skepticism are undermining the Christian faith of our youth, and the tendency in our Churches is to fashion and worldliness; and many professing Christians in high places of trust and responsibility, have disappointed the confidence of the public and stumbled the weak.

This, therefore, is no time for this Association to slacken its endeavors. And though other kindred associations are forming, and agencies multiplying to spread Scriptural holiness, *this Association* is the key-stone of the arch,—the head of the advancing column ! And God and the Church will hold this Association responsible for the solemn trust committed to it,—the maintenance of the doctrine and experience of a free and *full salvation.*

## " WHAT ARE THE OBLIGATIONS OF THE METHODIST MINISTRY TO THE DOCTRINE AND EXPERIENCE OF HOLINESS ?"*

### L. R. DUNN, D.D.

If I understand this question aright, it is not what the obligations of the class of persons referred to are to the doctrine and experience of holiness as taught in the word of God merely, but as that doctrine and experience are understood by the acknowledged and authoritative exponents of them in the M. E. Church. The former view would lead us to regard the question generally, and to show the obligations of *all* ministers of the gospel in relation to this doctrine and experience ; but the latter is specific and refers directly to the ministers of the M. E. Church. At first view, it would seem strange that there should exist any necessity for the consideration of such a question, after this doctrine and experience have been before the Church for more than a cen-

* This essay by Bro. Dunn was read at the afternoon session and should have been inserted on page 115.

tury : the one formulated in systems of divinity, in institutes, and sermons, and treatises, and commentaries, sung in the large majority of our standard hymns, preached by the fathers of the Church, in Europe, America, and to the uttermost parts of the earth ; and the other realized by thousands of our ministers and members, testified to in the love-feast and class-meeting, in life and in death, and recorded in the richest biographical literature possessed by any Church on the earth.

And yet, strange as it may sound and seem, the consideration of the question is by no means irrelevant or undemanded. Wide differences of sentiment are entertained and promulged in the Church, in volumes and treatises, and learned articles in our periodicals, and in sermons by which the minds of our ministry and people are confused, obscured, not to say blinded, upon this question. We venture the assertion, that any ordinary reader, carefully going over our standard authors, our biographies, and our hymns, would come to the following conclusions upon this question and its correlatives :

1. That justification is the free and full forgiveness of all our sins, the placing of the soul in a condition of reconciliation and peace with God, the dealing with us as if we had never sinned, and the dissolution of the liability to the penalties of the law denounced against transgressors.

2. That regeneration is the impartation of a new nature, a new life, by which we are enabled to live to God, to antagonize the remains of sin in our hearts, and to obey the commandments of God.

3. That thus justified and regenerated, we are adopted into the divine family, are recognized as children of God, and have the testimony of the Holy Spirit as to this blessed relation.

4. That entire sanctification, perfection, perfect love, entire holiness, is the complete removal of the remains of sin, by the

cleansing blood of Christ, and the mighty, transforming power of the Holy Ghost, so that nothing will exist hereafter in the soul—so long at least as its faith retains its perfect hold on Christ—contrary to the love of God. That this condition is not one of absolute, angelic, or Adamic perfection, not one from which there is no liability, or possibility, of falling, not one that delivers us from the involuntary effects of sin, such as, weaknesses, frailties, ignorances, short-comings, sicknesses, temptations, and death ; not one which renders us independent of the constant application of the cleansing blood and the abiding presence of the Comforter ; not one in which the Word of God, and prayer and all the means of grace are unnecessary; not one which admits of no further growth, and development of the soul, and its constant maturing in all the graces of the Holy Spirit.

Further, that this state, or experience, is to be attained, simply and solely, by faith in Christ, that it may be attained in this life—that at any time, when the soul is convinced of its *need* of this grace, or of its *privilege* to enjoy it—and will make a complete consecration of all its powers to God—and will believe that God will do this work, yea, that He *doeth it*, it will be done, and the Holy Spirit will bear His testimony to this fact.

These things, we say, will be readily learned by any one of ordinary intelligence, in a careful perusal of the works referred to. And yet, while he may *run* who readeth these things—so plainly and so constantly are they taught—many of our ministers and members, hold and teach views which directly or indirectly, antagonize these teachings upon the subject of Holiness. Some teach that the work of sanctification is entire and complete in regeneration—that no sin remains in the renewed heart ; thus not only putting themselves in antagonism to the Methodist doctrine upon this question of remaining sin, but, also, in opposition to the formulated dogmas of the whole Christian Church, in all the ages, with the exception only of the little sect of which Count Zinzendorf was the leader and the head.

Others teach that sin remains in the heart, and must and will there remain until death, but that divine grace will enable man to *repress* its tendencies, its strugglings for the mastery over the soul, and that its snake-heads are only spiked down, and are liable at any time to become loosened and thrust themselves through the character and the life. Others, again, teach that the work is *gradual*, and will increase more and more until, finally, grace will have such a mastery over the soul that sin will no longer pain us by its presence or bondage us with its power. Now all these views, whatever excellences they may have, or may seem to have in themselves, however honored and respected and pious those may be who hold and teach them, yet they are not the doctrines of the M. E. Church on this question; they, indeed, antagonize more or less that doctrine, and it is seemingly inconsistent for men to call themselves Methodists, and yet to practically discard the only distinguishing doctrine of Methodism. For, take away this doctrine from Methodism, and what are we, doctrinally, more than others? Wherein do we substantially differ from others? In what respect do we claim a *raison d'etre*, or a reason of existing as a separate and distinct denomination? Is it in the doctrine of God? Is it in the depravity of human nature? Is it in the necessity for and character of the atonement? It is, truly, in the extent of its application and appropriation, but, in nothing else, and even the *outcome* of our views on the *certainty* of God's plans and purposes, is the same as that of our Calvinistic brethren on the *necessity* of them. Is it in the nature and necessity of the new Birth? Is it even in the doctrine of the " Witness of the Spirit?" For this was taught clearly and strongly by many divines in the Post-reformation period before the time of Wesley. Is it in the agency and power of the Holy Ghost? Is it in the Resurrection, the Judgment—Heaven or Hell? No; in none of these things. But when we speak of the possibility of being cleansed from all sin, of being filled with the love of God, to the exclusion of the elements of sin remaining in the regenerate heart; of living without sin—in the sense of the transgression of the law, and of the conscious motions of sin in the soul—although not in the sense of frailties, weaknesses, and short-comings—of being thus saved in this life, we differ from all the other creeds of Evangelical Christendom, and in this alone, so far as *doctrines* are concerned, is found the reason of our existing as a separate and distinct denomination.

There were, doubtless, *individual* Christians in the Church of Rome, and in other Churches, who taught this doctrine and enjoyed this experience, as Marquis de Renty, Fenelon, Madame Guyon, Catherine Adorna, in the one, and Fox and Barclay among the Friends, and Payson, and Edwards and others in other Churches: but this *doctrine* is contained in no other creed in Christendom.

. To confirm this, I wish to quote from two of the leading minds of our Church, the heads of our two great Theological Institutions, the one still living, the other gone to be with God, Dr. M'Clintock, and Dr. Warren. No better or higher authority in our Church need be quoted than this:

"Knowing exactly what I say, and taking the full responsibility of it, I repeat we are the only Church in history, from the Apostles' time until now, that has put forward as its *elemental thought* the great central idea of the whole Book of God, from the beginning to the end,—*the holiness of the human soul, heart, mind and will.* Go through all the confessions of all the Churches, and you will find this in no other. It may be called fanaticism, but that, dear friends, is our mission. If we keep to that the next Century is ours. Our work is a moral work, that is to say, the work of making men holy. Our preaching is to that, our Church agencies are for that, our schools, colleges, universities and theological seminaries are for that. There is our mission. There is our glory. There is our power, and there shall be our triumph.*

In like manner Dr. Warren says : " In Luther's mind, justification by faith was the central idea of Christianity, and in Calvin's the decree was the central idea. But Methodism, in respect to its *inmost spirit and essence*, is a viewing of Christianity *from the stand-point of Christian Perfection or perfect love*. In Mr. Wesley's experience, the struggle was for *entire sanctification ;* and so, in the study of the doctrines of the Bible, he looked at them all from the higher stage of religious consciousness, and *perfect love* became the formal principle of his theology."† (The italics are our own).

"I know it may be said that I have misstated the question, as held by Wesleyan Methodism, that Mr. Wesley taught that sanctification is a *gradual* work, that his theory rather favored that of *repression* of sin, than a complete deliverance from sin, or that he taught we were sanctified wholly when we were regenerated."

And it is necessary, under the circumstances, that I should. prove to the contrary of all these statements. It may be admitted, that when Mr. Wesley talked, or wrote upon this general question, he was not always as guarded as he might have been. And it is unfair, from these general, and sometimes *loose* statements to gather up the teachings of our founder ; and the same thing is true of some other of our standard authors. The sources to which we are to look for evidence on this question are to those sermons, Institutes, treatises, etc., where the question is directly and definitely stated, and the doctrine most carefully formulated. And

* Dr. M'Clintock, Centenary Speech, St. Paul's, N. Y.
† Introduction to Theology.

when these sources are sought, there is no difficulty whatever in understanding the meaning of their words. It is to these formulated and definitive statements that I now call your attention. In the first place, I must, of course, call attention to the language of Mr. Wesley. He says, in a sermon preached at St. Mary's, Oxford, in 1733, before the University: " The circumcision of the heart is that habitual disposition of soul, which, in the sacred writings, is termed holiness; and which directly implies the being cleansed from sin, from all filthiness both of flesh and spirit ; and by consequence, the being endued with those virtues which were also in Christ Jesus; the being so renewed in the image of our mind, as to be perfect as our Father in heaven is perfect."

Thirty-two years after this, in 1765, he says of this sermon. " It contains all that I now teach concerning salvation from all sin, and loving God with an undivided heart." Wesley's Works, vol. 3 : p. 202 In that same sermon he taught that this holiness of heart is to be "*obtained alone by faith.*" As the doctrine of sin is a most important one in this connection, —he thus states definitely what he means by sin—when he says that we may be saved from all sin. "What do you mean by the word sin ? Do you mean those numberless weaknesses and follies, sometimes improperly termed sins of infirmity ? If so, we shall not put off these but with our bodies. But, if you mean that it—the Gospel Covenant—does not promise entire freedom from sin, in its proper sense, or from committing it, this is by no means true, unless the Scripture be false. Though it is possible a man may be a child of God, who is not fully freed from sin, it does not follow that freedom from sin is impossible; or that it is not to be expected by all. It is described by the Holy Ghost as *the common privilege of all.*" (Wesley, Preface to Life of Halyburton.) Again he says : "I never meant any *more* by perfection, than the loving God with all our heart, and serving Him with all our strength. But

I dare not say *less* than this. For it might be attended with worse consequences than you seem to be aware of. If there be a mistake it is far more dangerous on the one side than on the other. If I set the mark too high, I drive men into heedless fears; if you set it too low, you drive them into hell fire." (Meth. Mag. 1779, p. 475.)

These formulated statements might be multiplied, but time forbids my further notice of them.

I wish now to notice his clear and distinct utterances on the point that this state of holiness *is not the same as regeneration.* He says, speaking of the one who had obtained holiness, "It is not easy to conceive what a difference there is between that which he experiences now, and that which he experienced before. Till this universal change was wrought in his soul all his holiness was *mixed;* humility with pride, meekness with passion; love of God with love of creature; love of neighbor with some things contrary thereto and the will sometimes rebellious. His whole soul is now consistent with itself; there is no jarring string. All his passions flow in a continual stream, with an even tenor to God. There is no mixture of any contrary affections; all is peace and harmony after." Sermons, Vol. 2, p. 222. In his plain account he says in answer to the Ques. "When does inward sanctification begin? In the moment a man is justified. Yet sin remains in him, yea the seed of all sin, till he is sanctified throughout." P. 48–9. Mr. Watson says, "That a distinction exists between a regenerate state and a state of entire and perfect holiness will be generally allowed." Vol. 2, p. 450. In fact, to deny this, is to upturn the fundamental truths of our whole theological system. Mr. Wesley distinctly says in his Plain Account, "We do not know a single instance, in any place, of a person's receiving in one and the same moment remission of sins, the abiding witness of the Spirit, and a new, clean heart." P. 34. But does Mr. Wesley teach that this work is *gradual?* Yes: in the following sense: He says, "A child is born of a woman in a moment, or in a short time; afterwards he gradually and slowly grows, till he attains the stature of a man. In like manner, a child is born of God in a short time, if not in a moment. But, it is by slow degrees that he afterwards grows up to ' the measure of the fulness of Christ.' The same relation therefore which there is between our natural birth and our growth, there is also between our spiritual birth and our sanctification." Sermon. Vol. 1, p, 406. Mr. Wesley's, Vide Plain Account, p. 80-1, favorite illustration on this point however is this. "A man may be dying for some time, yet, he does not, properly speaking, die, till the instant the soul is separated from the body. And in that instant he lives the life of eternity. In like manner he may be dying to sin for some time, yet he is not dead to sin till sin is separated from his soul ; and in that instant he lives the full life of love. And as the change undergone when the body dies is of a different kind, and infinitely greater than any he had known before, yea, such as till then it is impossible to conceive, so the change wrought when the soul dies to sin is of a different kind, and infinitely greater than any before, and than any can conceive till he experiences it. Yet, he still grows in grace, in the knowledge of Christ, in the love and image of God : and will do so, not only till death, but to all eternity." Mr. Fletcher in like manner teaches both the gradualness and instantaneousness of this work. In answer to the question, " Is Christian perfection to be instantaneously brought down to us, or are we gradually to grow up to it?" he says, "Both ways are good—and supposes it possible that some believers have been gradually perfected—while he contends at the same time for the possible instantaneity of the work." Manual, p. 38 and 43. But, as Mr. Wesley advanced in life, and the witnesses of this great truth multiplied around him, he contended more earnestly for *full salvation now by faith*. Tyerman in his history, Vol. 2, p. 593, says, speaking of Mr. Wesley's Plain Account, "The book is really historical, rather than doctrinal, and is intended to show that Wesley's present views were substantially the views which he had held for the last forty years. This was unquestionably true, *with the one exception* of his now teaching, that Christian perfection is attainable in an *instant* and by faith only." Mr. Tyerman says, Mr. Wesley declares he began to teach this in 1741, eight years after his St. Mary's sermon. On the other hand Mr. Whitehead, in his life of Wesley, says he did not begin to teach it until 1760. In 1773 he wrote to John Bredin, "Strongly insist on full salvation to be received *now* by simple faith." In 1785 he wrote to F. Gamtsor, in America, "The more explicitly and strongly you press all believers to aspire after full sanctification as attainable now by simple faith, the more the whole work of God will prosper." Tyerman, Vol. 3, p. 462. To Rankin he wrote in 1774, "I have been lately thinking a good deal on one point wherein, perhaps, we have all been wanting. We have not made it a rule, as soon as ever persons are justified, to remind them of going on to perfection, whereas this is the very time preferable to all others."

It thus appears that Mr. Wesley and Mr Fletcher taught that all growth in grace in a regenerated person, is growth towards entire holiness, and that every faithful believer will thus grow; that there is, however, a point or period, when love is made perfect, so that nothing contrary thereto will exist in the soul; that, in many instances, this does not take place until at, or just before death; that death, however, is no factor in the purification of the heart; and, finally, on this point, that one may be made perfect in love, fully sanctified, cleansed from all sin, in an instant, at any time when faith grasps the provision and promise of God, and that growth is not, so much a question of time, as it is of the character and degree of our faith—both before and after entire sanctification. This must suffice as to the Methodist *doctrine* of Entire Sanctification.

What then about its *experience ?* Mr. Wesley says, Sermons, vol. 2, p. 223, " Four or five and forty years ago, when I had no distinct views of what the Apostles meant by exhorting us to leave the principles of the doctrine of Christ, etc., two or three persons in London whom I knew to be truly sincere, desired to give me an account of their experience. It appeared exceedingly strange, being different from any that I had heard before, but *exactly similar* to the preceding account of sanctification. The next year two or three, or more persons at Bristol and Kingwood, coming to me severally, gave me the same account of their experience. A few years later I desired all those in London, who made the same profession, to come to me altogether at the Foundry, that I might be thoroughly satisfied. When we met, first one of us (Thomas Walsh and himself), and then another, asked them the most searching questions we could devise. They answered every one without hesitation and with the utmost simplicity, so that we were fully persuaded they did not deceive themselves. In the years 1759-60-61-62 their numbers multiplied exceedingly, not only in London and Bristol, but in various parts of Ireland as well as England. Not trusting to the testimony of others, I carefully examined most of them myself, and in London alone I found 652 members of our society who were exceedingly clear in their experience, and of whose testimony I could see no reason to doubt. I believe no year has passed since that period wherein God has not wrought the same work in many others. And every one of these, I have not found one exception (after the most careful inquiry) either in Great Britain or in Ireland has declared that his deliverance from sin was *instantaneous*, that the change was wrought in a moment. Had half of these, or one-third, or one in twenty declared it was *gradually* wrought in them, I should have believed this with regard to *them,* and thought that *some* were gradually sanctified and some instantaneously. But, as I have not found, in so long a space of time, a *single person* speaking thus; as all who believe they are sanctified declare with one voice that the change was wrought in a moment, I cannot but believe that sanctification is, commonly, if not always, an *instantaneous* work." This you will see was towards the close of his life. This extract is long, but it is so valuable and clear that I have felt free to give it entire. This statement, here made, might be confirmed by a multitude of similar accounts in sermons, biographies and magazines. This then is clearly demonstrated that what was doctrinally taught by Mr. W. and his colaborers became a matter of clear, personal and conscious experience in hundreds and thousands of instances, so clear, so unmistakable, so perfectly convincing, that the logical mind of Mr. Wesley could find no flaws in that experience. Not only so. Many of the most prominent minds in the societies in England and America were clear and blessed witnesses of this truth and this experience. Fletcher and Bramwell, and Benson and Clarke, Whatcoat and Asbury, and Fish and Olin, among men ; and Mrs. Fletcher, Countess of Huntingdon, Lady Maxwell, Hester Ann Rogers, and Sarah Cowley, and afterwards Phœbe Palmer and a multitude of other women declared the wonderful things of God.

Such then are the doctrine and experience of holiness as taught and realized by multitudes in the Methodist Church. That some do not believe this doctrine is evident ; that many have not obtained this experience is evident; but this does not affect either. They stand immovably, and can never be expunged from the history of this wonderful movement, to "spread scriptural holiness over these lands."

These questions settled, it becomes an easy matter to answer the inquiry, "What are the obligations of the Methodist ministry to them?" To this I answer, 1st. They are under the most binding obligations to believe this doctrine without hesitation, or mental reservation. When a person connects himself with a Christian Church, it is with the avowed and understood confession, that he believes in its doctrines, and will submit to its discipline. The matter of joining a Christian Church *at all* is purely voluntary. No one is *compelled* to do this. No one is compelled to be a Methodist or a Methodist minister. And yet when one connects himself with the Methodist Church, voluntarily, and voluntarily enters its ministry, he ought to embrace cordially its doctrines, without any mental reservation. If he have doubts upon some of them, he should express them at the time of joining, or at the period of entering upon its ministry. Now suppose that this question was one that related to the doctrine of *Justification by faith.* And suppose one of our ministers to hold and teach that men are justified by works only; or, that there is no necessity for justification, or that men can only be justified at the last moment of their earthly existence, would we not all at once rise up to condemn such teachings, and say such a doctrine as that of being justified by works may do well enough for a Romanist; or that men do not need to be justified by Christ's blood, will answer for a Unitarian ; but neither of them will do for a Methodist. Now it would be easy to show that the standards of the Methodist Episcopal Church teach just as clearly the doctrine of entire sanctification by faith, as they do the doctrine of justification by faith. But for various reasons, there are ministers, some high in influence and authority, who speak slightingly of the doctrine and the experience, throw doubts upon the possibility of its being attained, caricature many who are its witnesses, and throw disabilities in the way of those who teach and preach it. And if some ministers and laymen among us could have their way, the doctrine would be expunged from our standards—banished from our pulpits, excerpted from our hymnology, and unheard of in our love-feasts and class-meetings. This is certainly very far from Mr. Wesley's idea and that of our fathers, of the responsibilities of Methodist ministers to the reception and proclamation of this truth.

2. Methodist ministers are under obligations to *preach this doctrine.* Mr. Wesley says: Plain Account, p. 169, "All our preachers should make a point of preaching perfection to believers, constantly, strongly and explicitly." And in almost numberless letters he distinctly declares in substance, that wherever this doctrine is preached, there the cause of God prospers; and where it is not there is decline, decay and death. To those preachers who had not obtained this grace he wrote: *preach it until you get it;* and to those who had, he said, *preach it because you have got it.* This, of course, does not imply that nothing else is to be preached but this. No; this is not to be hobbyized. So Mr. Wesley teaches, both by precept and example. No man ever preached or wrote upon a greater variety of subjects than he did. But, it is to have that place in our preaching that it has in the word of God, that it has in the standards and hymnology of our Church, *that it has in the cross of our Lord Jesus Christ.* This is indeed the grand central idea of Christianity. Around it all other truths revolve in harmony, without it, all other truths become, sooner or later, dim, misty, shadowy, uncertain. But there is a great difference in the *manner* of preaching this truth. Some proclaim it as a theory, and merely from a sense of duty, others modify it, and eliminate from it all its essence and power; others preach it harshly, censoriously, dogmatically and uncharitably. The only really *effective* method of preaching it is from the stand-point of experience, and with the Spirit of the gentle and loving Jesus. Men are not to be scolded, argued, driven, or brow-beaten into this doctrine or experience, but we are to speak this, as all other truth, in love. This great truth has suffered, almost irreparably, by the man-

ner in which many have preached it. And yet Methodist preachers, to be consistent, *must preach it.* If I may be allowed a little personal experience upon this point, I would say, that for years I occasionally preached this doctrine as a theory. I felt it to be my duty, as a Methodist preacher, so to do. Some of the best sermons which I have on this subject, I wrotre before I obtained the grace of which I spoke. And, I may add, I always felt that God blessed me when I proclaimed this truth. But, it was a different thing after I had experienced it. I *knew* then the truth, which before was only a theory, and, sometimes, very loosely held.

3. It is the *duty* of *every Methodist Minister* to *experience this great blessing.* It is a fact, well known, that *every one* of our ministers, before he is admitted to be ordained as a minister, is required to answer affirmatively the following questions: "Are you going on to perfection? Do you expect to be made perfect in love in this life? Are you groaning after it?" Dis. p. 149. These questions must be answered affirmatively, or else the candidate will be arrested on the very threshold of his ministry, and refused ordination. *But what does all this mean?* Is this a mere form? Is it a solemn farce? Are men to answer these questions affirmatively and then, turning their backs upon the altars of the Church, go out the next moment and say, "I don't believe in Christian perfection?" Or, go out into the work of the ministry and never preach upon the subject, except to caricature it, and those who believe it, and experience it? And, instead of *groaning* after it, as an object infinitely worthy to be desired, discouraging any mention of it in the social meetings of the Church? Surely, if these words mean anything; aye if these *solemn vows* mean anything, then they mean that perfect love is a great truth of God's word, so clearly revealed that we know its name and know what it means, so firmly believed that we expect to obtain and enjoy it *in this life,* and so earnestly desired that

we are *groaning* after it. It means all this, or it means nothing at all, it is only a solemn farce. More solemn and serious would it be, if the leaders of our institutions should exhaust their stock of knowledge and genius in attempts to tone down these truths in the presence of candidates for the ministry and paralyze all efforts to obtain this grace, and discourage all promptings to testify to its reality, its preciousness and its power.

If this doctrine and this experience are to be treated thus, then Methodism is a meaningless thing, our biographical literature deserves the fate it is receiving—of lying dusty and unread upon the shelves of our book depositories—and a large part of our hymns ought, at once, to be obliterated from our hymn-book. We should be honest at least, and consistent with ourselves, and either brand the doctrine and experience as obsolete and untrue; or else perform our ordination vows, and groan after this perfect love until it is obtained. And, certainly, if we are *groaning* after it, it will not be long before we feel its grace and power. And yet, I conceive, we should ever have and manifest the kindliest feelings for those who differ from us on this question, remembering, as we ever should, that there was a time in our history and experience when we thought and felt very differently from what we now do. There have always been differences of opinion and expression among our ministers on this subject, even in Mr. Wesley's day. Nothing is to be gained by traducing the character or motives of our brethren, nor by segregating ourselves from them. While I am convinced of these obligations of the Methodist ministry, I am satisfied that many in their interpretations of the Wesleyan doctrine, honestly differ from me. I cannot doubt either their piety or sincerity, and I only pray that the Holy Spirit may show them, as He did me, the true meaning of this doctrine and experience. In his Plain Account, p. 147, Mr. W. says: "Beware of schism, in making a rent in the Church of Christ. That inward disunion, the members ceasing to have a reciprocal love for one another, is the very root of all contention, and of every outward separation. Beware of everything tending thereto. Beware of a dividing spirit; shun whatever has the least aspect that way. Therefore say not, 'I am of Paul, or of Apollos'; the very thing which occasioned the schism at Corinth. Do not despise or run down any preacher; do not exalt any one above the rest, lest you hurt both him and the cause of God. On the other hand, do not bear hard upon any by reason of some incoherency or inaccuracy of expression; no, nor for some mistakes, were they really such." With the spirit and language of this quotation I cordially agree. Let me say then in closing these remarks: Above all things else, we need this doctrine and experience at the present hour. For want of a holy Church—founded upon the principles of Bible holiness—the world has been gradually encroaching upon Zion, not only treading in its outer courts, and there clamoring for recognition; but it has pressed up to its very altars and holy places, and flaunted its banners in them. It has aimed to rule all spirituality out of the Church. It has demanded that no special interest should be manifested in religion. It has branded all religious zeal as fanaticism. It has bade the pulpits not to quake with Sinai's thunders, nor to blaze with its lightnings. It will not tolerate the mention of holiness. It will not allow its theatres, operas, dances, and drinking customs to be denounced—yea, it demands that the Church should recognize them, in part at least, by adopting them substantially, as a part of its own regime.

And what is the fruitage we have been reaping from yielding, at least in a measure to these demands? Peculations, frauds, impurities, looseness of the marital vows, ante-natal murders, such a slaughter of innocents as the world never

knew before—coldness, barrenness, spiritual death in many
forms, and in many places, intemperance, running rampant,
shouting in bacchanalian revelry and triumph over the groans,
sighs, tears, murders, riots, crimes, sicknesses, it occasions, and
the slaughter of many thousands annually by its power. And
Romanism, seeing but too clearly the decadence of the real
vitality of Protestantism, is stealthily laying its iron grasp upon
the very throat of American liberties, gaining control in all
our large cities, shutting out the Bible from our schools and
preparing to place the government of this country under its
bloody iron hoof and heel. All these things have come upon
us, and yet we are not awakened out of our stupor or alarmed
for our safety. No nation that has ever existed upon this
globe has had, or has now such light, such privileges, such
advantages and such opportunities. And no Church, in
any period of the world's history, ever had such light, such
truth, such preaching, such hymns, such biographies, such
privileges and possibilities as the Methodist Church has enjoyed. We have had the light, we *have* the light; and "if
the light, which is in us be darkness, how great is that darkness?" Dr. Olin, well remarked, as true in his own experience and in that of others, that if this great truth is not firmly
held by our ministers, a mist will come over our minds and
hearts, and we shall grope in the darkness. The Ministry of
the Methodist Episcopal Church cannot afford to ignore this
doctrine, to antagonize it, to tone it down, to emasculate it.
Such a course will not only bring leanness into our own souls,
but leanness into our Churches, and will grieve the Holy Spirit.
We have had all the advantages of all the increasing light
which has been shed upon the sacred page in the 19th Century. We have had all the teachings furnished us by the
Lutheran Reformation.

Mr. Wesley's first Christian experience was kindled at the
altar of Luther's exegesis. We have learned all that was val-

uable in Calvin's theology, and nearly battled the balance out
of existence. Our history has been contemporaneous with,
and, indeed, in many instances, inseparably associated with
all the benevolent and forward movements of the Church,
missionary, Bible, tract, Sunday-School. We have not only
in our standards, the distinctively Pauline doctrine of justification by faith, but also, the Johannine doctrine of perfect
love, a truth that neither Augustine, nor Calvin, nor Luther at
all apprehended. Starting out from this grandest truth of God's
word, and from this highest point of Christian experience, we
have been singing hymns of full salvation from all sin, now
experienced by faith, all around the globe, and such revivals
have followed as the world never saw or knew before. And
now are we to lower our banners, and trail them in the dirt?
Are we to deny, or to be ashamed of, those weapons before which
the infidelity of Rousseau, Bolingbroke, Hume, and Tom
Paine went down; before which the sepulchres of a dead formalism were opened, and the lifeless corpse of a buried Christianity heard the voice of the Son of God saying, Resurgam,
Arise and shine for thy light is come; and the glory of the
Lord has risen upon them, before which millions of immortal
beings, in England, Ireland, Scotland, Wales, America, the
West India Islands, Australia, China, and the Islands of the
Sea, have bowed into the dust of penitence, and then risen up
in the glory of redemption and regeneration? God forbid
it! Rather let us seize anew the standard and bear it aloft
everywhere. Let us bear in mind that nothing but a divine
religion, which *is, and always must be*, a holy religion, can
save our humanity. O, if the Methodist Church were only
true to her mission, of spreading scriptural holiness over these
and all lands, if there were less scramble for position, office,
and power, less grasping after the world, less assimilation to
the world, we should shake this nation from ocean to ocean,
and fill it with hosannas and hallelujahs, we should throw our

altar lights athwart the gloom of every system of heathenism. Instead of our missionary treasury being in debt to an alarming amount—in expending a little more than half a million for the conversion of the world—we should annually contribute millions for this cause; we should throttle the giant foe of intemperance and crush him into the dust, with the aid of our brethren of other Churches who would catch the same holy flame, and Romanism, checkmated, baffled, counterworked, blasted and blinded, would fall down like another Dagon before the ark of the Lord. Well may we cry out, as in the Veni Creator Spiritus, which we utter responsively in our ordination service

> " Come Holy Ghost, our souls inspire,
> And lighten with celestial fire.
> Thou the anointing Spirit art,
> Who dost Thy seven-fold gifts impart.
> Thy blessed unction from above,
> Is comfort, light, and fire of love.
> Enable with perpetual light
> The darkness of our blinded sight.
> Anoint and cheer our soiléd face
> With the abundance of Thy grace.
> Keep far our foes, give peace at home,
> Where Thou art guide no ill can come.
> Teach us to know the Father, Son,
> And Thou of both to be but one;
> That thro' the ages all along,
> This may be our endless song,
> Praise to Thy eternal merit,
> Father, Son, and Holy Spirit."

On Thursday, A. M., the 12th, Bro. Inskip led a meeting for consecration and prayer. It was a season of remarkable unction and power. The altar was crowded with seekers for the baptism of fire. And the fire came. Many were gloriously saved.

At 10½, Bro. J. A. Wood read an essay on

# IN WHAT SENSE IS SANCTIFICATION GRADUAL, AND IN WHAT SENSE IS IT INSTANTANEOUS?

**REV. J. A. WOOD.**

Christian sanctification involves two principal items—*consecration* and *purification*. Consecration alone, is not purification ;—it precedes it, and always accompanies it.

Entire sanctification is a state of entire consecration attended with *purification*, through the soul-cleansing power of the Holy Ghost.

We maintain that sanctification, or *heart-purity*, wrought in the soul in part in regeneration, and completed in entire sanctification, strictly speaking is *instantaneous* and *never gradual*.

The Christian life, as it respects culture, development,— the growth of Christian virtues and maturity, we admit to be gradual, and never instantaneous. It should be borne in mind, that *purity* and *maturity* are widely different things. The destruction and removal of inbred sin, and the growth of the new life in Christ are not identical, and should not be confounded.

This view we might sustain by the highest authorities of the Church ; but will only present a clause from the excellent work of Dr. George Peck, on Christian Perfection. He says,—" It will be remembered, that we have found sanctification to imply both the *death of sin* and the *life of righteousness*. And when we speak of entire sanctification, as to the former part of it (the death of sin), we say it may be obtained at once—*it is an instantaneous work.*

But in relation to the latter part of this great work, viz. : the life of righteousness, embracing all holy affections, and pious efforts, it is regarded as *entirely progressive.*"——"*The destruction of sin in the soul* and *the growth of holiness are two distinct things.*" "The one is instantaneous, the other gradual; and hence it is that we sometimes say, with propriety, that the work of entire sanctification is both gradual and instantaneous."

Entire sanctification, in so far as it involves devotement, or entire consecration to God, is progressive and has its stages and gradual approach to the mind's apprehension of duty.

All the preparatory steps to the reception of entire sanctification are *gradual;* and the *development* of entire sanctification in the life is gradual.

Sanctification, as it stands related to the soul's *activities;* and the formation of our *habitudes* and a *faultless life*, must be gradual. Purity related to our voluntary powers, and holding their action in complete harmony with the will of God, must necessarily progress with increasing light and spiritual vigor. But, while what precedes and follows purification are gradual, the specific, supernatural, divine work of cleansing the heart, is *instantaneous.*

We allow that growth in grace, culture, development, and sanctified habits, will secure increasing light, and afford increasing power to overcome and hold in subjection remaining inbred sin, though they do not *eradicate* it, or *cleanse* the heart. While they may abate its force, they cannot change its nature, or remove it from the soul.

*Growth in grace is not a cleansing process.* The soul's increasing strength affords easier victories *over* depravity, but cannot exterminate it, or cleanse the soul. The *subjugation* of indwelling sin is not its extermination, or removal; and growth in grace, which contemplates the subjugation only of inbred sin is no definite approach to entire sanctification.

Increasing light will reveal more clearly the remaining deformity and impurity in the heart, though it does not remove it, as light cannot shine inbred sin out of the heart. An increase of patience will afford a more easy and complete victory over impatience; but that does not remove inbred sin,—the cause of the tendency to impatience, which inheres in the soul, and cannot be removed by the mere increase or improvement of any grace. An increase of love will secure a more easy and complete victory over all its antagonisms in the heart, but that does not destroy or remove the cause of these *inward, sinward tendencies.* The same is true of every other grace of the Christian life.

"Moral depravity (says Bishop Hamline), is not in *action* or *deed,* but lies further back, and deeper down in our nature, at the fountain head of all activity or character." See Sermon on Depravity.

This original, inborn sin, cannot be gradually and imperceptibly grown out, without a supernatural, instantaneous operation of the Holy Spirit.

Sanctification is no *natural* work, it is no *inner process* of nature like growth in the vegetable, or animal kingdom.

By growth in grace we may increase in knowledge; habits of virtue may strengthen; the graces of the Spirit to some extent may become more and more mature, established, and fortified, and thus inbred sin may be stunned, its power lessened, and its operations prevented; while the soul is yet unsaved from its inbeing and existence.

Its removal is an *instantaneous*—not a *gradual* work, a *divine,* not a *human* work. The soul is *passive* in purification;—it is the *subject,* not the *agent* of the cleansing. It is active, and co-operative with what precedes, and with what follows the cleansing; but the cleansing itself, is something *experienced,* and not something *done* by the soul.

In repentance, confession, humiliation, consecration, faith, and in all active duties, the powers of the soul are called into exercise, and are not passive.

The soul is passive in being cleansed, as it was in regeneration. Both are God's work. Both are supernatural. Both are conditional, involving human agency, and are not accomplished by secondary or natural causes.

Regeneration and sanctification are predominantly referred to the Holy Spirit in the Scriptures, as His peculiar work. While rites, sacraments, truths, and means of grace are all proper, necessary and useful, they cannot cleanse the heart, either in whole or in part.

Secondary causes and influences are utterly inefficient to purify the soul; that is God's work. These secondary causes may help us to God, and aid us in reaching the conditions of the divine work.

Bishop Foster says: "This work is of God entirely. These means do nothing; they only bring you to God, and He sanctifies; without them you cannot come to God, and unless you come He cannot sanctify; but *your coming does not sanctify*, it brings you to Him who does."—*Christian Purity. Page* 219.

Rev. Timothy Merritt, in his "Manual on Christian Perfection," describes the gradual process thus: "The gradations may be as follows: 1st. Light is imparted to the soul. 2d. Conviction is fastened upon the conscience. 3d. A desire springs up to be delivered from all sin. 4th. He confesses and prays for deliverance. 5th. He is convinced that he cannot cleanse his own heart, and therefore casts himself on the mercy of God for this. 6th. *The work is wrought in him.* Now it is evident that these several actions may be performed in a short time."

If this process be correct, as given by the sainted Merritt, and we maintain that it is, how clear that the soul is not being sanctified or purified at all, during what is called the gradual process, or during the first five items stated. Obtaining light, receiving conviction, hungering after purity, and confession and prayer, are in no sense the work of sanctifying the soul. They may each exist, and the soul remain unsanctified.

Receiving light may expel our darkness, but does not cleanse our pollution. It may reveal our inbred sin, and the remedy for it; but it cannot make us pure. It reveals the blood of Christ which can. The items named precede purification, but they do not affect it, and they certainly do not constitute its identity.

The sinner passes through a similar process before his regeneration; but no one claims that his receiving light, and conviction, his confession, prayers, and penitence regenerate his soul. They only precede that work, and are associated with its conditional cause.

Purity is the result of a cleansing wrought in the soul itself, (and not in its actions or exercises) by the Holy Ghost. In the very nature of the case, the soul must be sanctified by some other force, than the natural laws of development, culture and growth, as these are powerless to remove impurity from the heart. No *degree* of these can purify the heart, which involves a *purgation*, an *ablution*—an *extermination*, a *destruction* or *death*.

We present the following arguments in proof of the *instantaneousness* of sanctification:—

1. This grace is not achieved by the believer over *outward* enemies, but is wrought in us, by the removal of an inherent depravity;—a purification, not by warfare and successive victories *over depravity*, but by the Holy Ghost. The Christian warfare is both necessary and useful, but is not a *cleansing process*. There is no Christian effort or exercise, which can purge the soul from sin, and the Scriptures nowhere teach, that the gradual advances of a Christian by consecutive steps, or acts of obedience, are attended by a gradual cleansing of the heart, stain after stain departing, till all impurity is gone. .

Retrenchment, pruning, and lopping off excrescences of the outer life, purify no man's heart. The nature of a tree cannot be changed by pruning it. Make the tree good, and the branches will be good; then they will bear good fruit. God does His work in the heart and not at a man's fingers to save him, and make him a saint. He does not begin at the outer man, and cleanse his activities, but goes directly to the heart—the fountain whence all corrupt streams flow, and cleanses it. Having done His work there, He says: *"Now are ye clean."*

2. We argue an instantaneous purification from the figures used in the Scriptures significant of purity—those used to define and enforce it. They all teach that purification is a short and rapid work. Every one of them imply rapidity and dispatch.

1st Instance—*Death by crucifixion.* "Knowing this, that our old man is crucified with him, that the body of sin might be destroyed." Rom. 6 : 6. Mr. Benson says:—"Our old man, signifies our entire depravity and corruption, which by nature spreads itself over the whole man, leaving no part uninfected." *Crucifixion is a short process.*

2d. *Death by mortification.* "Mortify, therefore, your members which are upon the earth." Col. 3: 5. Let mortification commence, and go forward, and it will soon lay its victim in the dust.

3d. *The process of Creation.* "Create in me a clean heart, O God." "And that ye put on the new man, which after God is *created* in righteousness and true holiness." The process of creation so far as we know is instantaneous.

4th. *The cleansing of the leper.* "Purge me with hyssop, and I shall be clean." Leprosy was incurable by human means, and its cure was only effected by a *special work of God,* and effected in a moment. The cleansing of the leper was an emblem of the removal of sin, and indicated an instan-

taneous work. The whole process was short. Christ said,—
"I will, be thou clean, and immediately his leprosy was
cleansed."—Math. 8: 3.

5th. *The refinement of silver and gold.* "I will turn my
hand upon thee, and purely purge away thy dross, and take
away all thy tin." This is another short process, in which
Christ is likened to a "refiner and purifier of silver."

6th. *The working of leaven.* "The kingdom of heaven is
like unto leaven, which a woman took and hid in three measures of meal until the whole was leavened." Here again is a
short work, not exceedingly twelve hours. The parable is
plain, simple and adapted to the weakest capacity.

7th. *It is represented as an ablution.* "Wash me and I shall
be whiter than snow." "Then will I sprinkle clean water
upon you and ye shall be clean, &c." This figure, so common
and so significant, indicates a short process.

In harmony with these Bible figures, all the commands,
invitations and promises of God, respecting holiness, are in
the present tense. They are as clearly, as *strictly* and *definitely*
so, as those to the sinner regarding repentance, obedience,
justification and regeneration. In point of time, their united
language is, "Behold, *now* is the accepted time, behold, *now*
*is the day of salvation.*" God desires, commands and expects instant obedience. This cannot be done if sanctification is a gradual process. God commands—"Be ye holy,"
"Be ye filled with the Spirit," "Be ye therefore perfect,"—
"This is the will of God even your sanctification," and
"Thou shalt love the Lord, thy God, with all thy heart."
Just as surely as God desires and commands us *now* to "be
holy," *now* to "be perfect," and *now* to "love him with all
our heart;" so surely are sin's destruction and heart purification instantaneous.

3d. We maintain, that as sanctification is by faith, it must
be instantaneous—a short, rapid, quick work the same as
regeneration.

Purification *by faith*, is the universal doctrine of the Church of God. Mr. Wesley says,—"I have continually testified (for these five and twenty years) in private and public, that we are sanctified as well as justified by faith. And, indeed, the one of those great truths does exceedingly illustrate the other. *Exactly as we are justified by faith, so are we sanctified by faith.*" Works, Vol. I., p. 133.

"The work proper of cleansing the heart from sin (says Dr. F. G. Hibbard) is the work of God, always wrought through faith."

Rev. Dr. Fuller, of the Baptist Church, said in his address before the Evangelical Alliance, "Nor did you find relief, peace, strength, victory over your corruptions until you repaired to the fountain open for sin and uncleanness, until looking to Jesus, just as you did at first for pardon." He further added, "That in subduing our depravities, one act of faith is worth a whole life of attempted faithfulness."

Dr. George Smith, F. S. A., a distinguished author, says : "And as we obtained pardon by simple faith in Jesus, so must we obtain purity. We are no more able to work out the latter in our own hearts than the former. One is as fully purchased for us by the blood of Jesus, and as freely promised to us as the other. We must come then to the great and precious promises, and exercise a faith precisely analogous to that by which we were justified."—*Lectures on Theology*.

Experience teaches that man is as positively saved from the pollution of sin by faith in the cleansing blood of Christ, as that he is saved from the guilt of sin by faith in the pardoning mercy of God. The faith by which he is justified has regard to the promise of pardon, while the faith by which he is wholly sanctified has respect to the promise of cleansing. It is clear that the Scriptures give the same encouragement to the one as to the other. In both cases it is the same reliance on the promise of God, and differing only in the object for which it trusts.

The beautiful analogy in the conditions and experience of regeneration and entire'sanctification, teaches an instantaneous santification similar to regeneration. The sinner believes evangelically for pardon, and is forgiven, *freely* and fully. The Christian believes evangelically for holiness, and his heart is made *pure, entirely* and *instantaneously*. Each receives what he seeks and believes in Christ for.

Purity being by faith, being God's work, and wrought in the soul by His almighty power, it is reasonable to suppose, like its kindred blessings, pardon, regeneration and adoption, it is instantaneous rather than gradual.

The reception of that which is conditioned on faith, can only be obtained by believing for it ; and we can believe for only what we *see* and *feel* the need of. Hence, light, conviction and conscious need, must precede evangelical faith for the reception of any divinely promised blessing.

4th. We maintain that the uniform experience of all who are clear in the light of personal holiness, teaches that entire sanctification is instantaneously wrought.

So far as I know, experience uniformly teaches that purity is the result of a direct exercise of divine power, received as instantaneously as regeneration :—" *Sanctified by the Holy Ghost.*"

Three things are distinct in this experience : 1st. There is a consciousness of inbred sin after conversion. 2d. There is conviction of the privilege and duty of being cleansed from sin, and made pure in heart. 3d. It is personally sought and obtained as an instantaneous cleansing in the blood of Christ. These three items will be found, we believe, in every clear and definite experience of Christian purity.

Our experience and observation harmonize with the statement of Mr. Wesley: "In London alone I found six hundred and fifty-two members of our society, *who were exceeding clear in their experience*, and of whose testimony I could see no reason to doubt." "And *every one* of these (after the most careful inquiry, I have not found *one exception* in Great Britain or Ireland,) has declared that his deliverance from sin was instantaneous; that the change *was wrought in a moment.* Had half of these, or one-third, or one in twenty, declared it was gradually wrought in them, I should have believed this in regard to them, and thought that some were *gradually sanctified*, and some *instantaneously*. But as I have not found, in so long a space of time (more than thirty years), a single person speaking thus, *as all*, who believe they are sanctified, declare with one voice, that the change was wrought in a moment, I cannot but believe, that sanctification is commonly, if not always, an instantaneous work." Sermons, vol. 2, p. 223.

Bishop Janes, in a sermon at Morristown, New Jersey, said: "Well, now, what shall we do when Fletcher and Benson, and Bramwell and David Stoner, Dr.'s Fisk and Olin, and Bangs, and tens of thousands of others have testified, both in life and in death, that they are conscious of the *hour* and the *place*, when God, by the Holy Ghost, cleansed them from all unrighteousness."

Rev. Henry Bœhm gives an account of the work of God in the days of Asbury,—in the following statements taken from his diary: "There were one hundred and forty-six converted and seventy-six sanctified during the day." "At sunset they reported three hundred and thirty-nine conversions and one hundred and twenty-two sanctifications." "Peter Vannost preached at eight o'clock; eighty-one converted that evening, and sixty-eight sanctified." "There were this day two hundred and sixty-four conversions and fifty sanctifications." "There were one thousand one hundred conversions and nine hundred and sixteen sanctifications" during the meeting. Here we have the work of God, plainly stated in the old Methodist way, by the sainted Bœhm, who was an eye-witness and participator in the meetings he reports.

From the diaries, journals, magazines, biographies, and histories of Methodism during a hundred years past, several thousand quotations might be given like the foregoing from Father Bœhm.

In the great revival of holiness during the past twelve years, this blessing has been sought and obtained by simple faith in the blood of Christ, and enjoyed and testified to as a personal experience by Christians of all denominations, and in every walk of life. Thousands of Methodists, Baptists, Congregationalists, Presbyterians, Episcopalians, Quakers, and others in both Europe and America, have given their testimony to this experience.

And, brethren, it has been the chief honor of our denomination, that it has led thousands and thousands into the light and enjoyment of this most precious grace, whose lives have been beautiful and fragrant with whatever is " pure, lovely, and of good report."

So far as I know this great "cloud of witnesses" have given testimony to an instantaneous work of the blessed Holy Ghost—a work of *purification* and not of *maturity.*

This testimony has been given through a long succession of years; given by living, intelligent, competent witnesses, given in prosperity and in adversity, in sickness and in health, living and dying; and there is no power in earth or in hell that can impeach it.

Notwithstanding all this, with many we fear sanctification, is confounded with culture, development and growth in grace, and they expect to be sanctified in that way. This is a very serious mistake. Growth and development, are not the process of *refining, judging,* or *separating* sin from the soul, either before, or after entire sanctification. Doctor Hodge, of Princeton, in his Systematic Theology, well says: " *Nor is sanctification to be confounded with the effects of moral culture or discipline."* He further adds it is not by a "mere process of moral culture, by moral means; it is as truly *supernatural in its methods* as in its *nature."*

Growth, culture and development, and all *gradual processes* appertain to the "new man," to the "new life in Christ," and not to the *destruction* of carnal nature, and should not be mixed with the supernatural process of purification in "perfecting the saints."

Growth and development have no fixed relations to *purity* in any way. They have respect to *size* or *enlargement,* and not to *purity* or *quality.* Growth never changes the *nature* of anything; hence a believer cannot grow pure, on the same ground, or principle, that a sinner cannot grow into a saint— growth not changing the *nature* of things. A pure nature may grow, and an impure one may grow, and mere growth does not change the one or the other.

All changes by growth and development—by gradual processes are in *size* or *quantity,* and not in *mind* or *quality.* Purity has respect to *quality,* and not to *size* or *quantity.*

Hear John Wesley. He says: "You may obtain a growing *victory over* sin from the moment you are justified. *But this is not enough.* The body of sin, the *carnal mind,* must be *destroyed;* the old man must be slain; or we cannot put on the new man, which is created after God (or which is the image of God) in righteousness and true holiness, and *this is done in a moment.* TO TALK OF THIS BEING GRADUAL, would be nonsense as much as if we talked of a gradual justification." Journal of Hester Ann Rogers, p. 174.

Again he says, "As to manner, I believe this perfection is *always* wrought in the soul by a simple act of faith; consequently in an instant."

Bishop Jesse T. Peck said at Round Lake, "There is not a word of truth in it, and it is a serious mistake to trust to growing into a state of purity. God has exhausted the Bible symbols to get before us the idea, that is exactly opposite of the process of growth ; viz. that sin can be really taken out, and this is the reason why we are urging you to have it done to day."—*Penuel.*

Dr. Nathan Bangs says : "Those who teach that we are gradually to grow into a state of sanctification, without ever experiencing an instantaneous change from inbred sin to holiness,—are to be repudiated as unsound—anti-scriptural and anti-Wesleyan."—*Articles in Guide.*

Dr. Adam Clarke says: "In no part of the Scriptures are we directed to seek holiness by gradation. We are to come to God as well for an instantaneous and complete purification from all sin, as for an instantaneous pardon. Neither a seriatim pardon, nor the gradation purification, exists in the Bible."—*Clarke's Theology,* .*p* 208.

We conclude with the following clear statement from Mr. Wesley : "Indeed, this is so evident a truth, that well nigh all the children of God scattered abroad, however they differ in other points, yet generally agree in this : That although we may, by the Spirit mortify the deeds of the body ; resist and conquer both outward and inward sin ; although we may weaken our enemies day by day ;—yet we cannot drive them out. By all the grace which is given at justification, we cannot extirpate them. Though we watch and pray ever so much, we cannot wholly cleanse either our hearts or hands. Most sure we cannot till it shall please our Lord to speak to our hearts again, to speak the second time, be clean ; and then only the leprosy is cleansed. Then only the evil root, the carnal mind, is destroyed ; and indeed sin subsists no more.

But if there be no such second change, if there be no instantaneous deliverance after justification, if there be none but a gradual work of God (that there is a gradual work none denies), then we must be content, as well as we can to remain full of sin till death."—*Sermons, vol.* 1, *p.* 122.

The paper and discussion that followed it gave much clear light to this difficult question.

An interesting feature of the Convention was the answering of questions pertaining to all the phases of the theory and practice of holiness. Here are a few specimens:

"How shall we infallibly distinguish between the voice of God speaking in us and our own imagination?"

Answer by Bro. Inskip: "I know no way but by referring to the word of God."

"Is there such a thing as getting such an abiding sense of Jesus' presence as not to hunger and thirst?"

Answer by Bro. Parker: "When you are as large as God, you will cease to hunger after Him, and not before."

"Does the Holy Ghost, in entire sanctification, work separate from the truth?"

Answer by Bro. Parker: "Never; no, never."

"Is it advisable for professors of entire sanctification in Churches where they are in sufficient numbers to do so, to hold meetings for that specific object?"

Answer by Bro. Inskip: "I have no kind of doubt that it is both necessary and proper. But in no case to interfere with the regular operations of the Church."

"If we know by faith that Christ dwells in our hearts in His fulness as an abiding presence, and are conscious of that presence, are we justified in calling for Him in strong cries and tears to come?"

Answer by Bro. Wood: "We *receive* by faith. We *know* by experience. We are justified in strong cries and tears for a richer baptism of the Holy Gost."

"How does the Holy Spirit lead us, or how may we know that we are led by the Holy Spirit to say or do things to others?

Answer by Bro. Macdonald : " Holiness does not make us infallible. We must use our judgments, and may not always be correct. We cannot trust to impressions. The word of God must harmonize with our impressions."

" Is there more than one baptism of the Holy Spirit?"

Answer by Bro. Macdonald: "There is one baptism of the Holy Spirit, and that is in sanctification, but we have greater waves coming in on the soul."

There were many precious pearls gathered up during these hours of question and reply which will be invaluable to the experience and practice of perfect love in those who enjoyed them.

At the afternoon session Rev. Alex. McLean read an essay on

## DOES THE WESLEYAN DOCTRINE OF ENTIRE SANCTIFICATION PRESENT INSUPERABLE DIFFICULTIES TO A SUBSTANTIAL AGREEMENT AMONG METHODISTS ?

REV. ALEX. M'LEAN.

To the many who are worthy to bear the name of Methodist, there are but few and slight doctrinal hindrances in the way of receiving the theory, or possessing the experience of Christian perfection. To come to God with the simplicity of a little child, to be led by the Spirit into all truth, will effectually dispel the difficulties. Christ will enable us to walk in the light, as He is in the light. Indeed to those who are born of the Spirit, it is easier to enter into the holy of holies of entire sanctification than it is for the unconverted to pass into the conscious assurance of justification. It is alleged " Methodists are agreed as to the doctrine. It is only as to the methods employed to spread the experience of heart purity, about which there is substantial disagreement." We fear this is but a sad evidence that with such ob-

8

jectors the chief difficulty is a hostility to the grace, which lies not so much in the head as it is deep seated in the heart. It may be so imbedded in the soul as to escape a casual observation. Think of Paul's objecting to the course pursued by brethren in the different Churches, who were gaining many firm adherents to the cross of Christ, because of the methods employed ; when of these it could only be said they were new, and against them not the slightest insinuation of impropriety was whispered.

Church history shows no one denomination to have resorted to more expedients in the same length of time to propagate a pure gospel than have the Methodists. Objections to methods are about as old as the carnal mind, and they have been levelled against every earnest endeavor to hasten the answer of the prayer, "Thy will be done on Earth as it is in Heaven." A thousand times repeated has been the assaults on methods, even when the sole effort has been to turn the ungodly from the way of death eternal. Dr. C. G. Finney, whose success as an evangelist was as marked as his Christian candor was appreciated, said, "If we examine the history of the Church we shall find that there never has been an extensive reformation except by new measures. * * * The present cry against new measures is highly ridiculous when we consider the quarter from which it comes, and all the circumstances in the case." He continues, "It is truly astonishing that grave ministers should really feel alarmed at the new measures of the present day, as if new measures were new under the sun ; and as if the present form and manner of doing things had descended from the Apostles and were established by a 'thus saith the Lord,' when the truth is that every step of the Church's advance, from the gross darkness of Popery, has been through the introduction of one new measure after another."

As we cannot believe there is any enduring sincerity in

the objections, urged never so vehemently, against methods and measures, we pass on to inquire: *Wherein do Methodists essentially differ about Christian perfection ?* We speak of this denomination particularly (1) because from the very beginning it has been affirmed they were raised up to spread Scriptural holiness over these lands. (2) Because no denomination ever gave to it so exhaustive an inquiry; or formulated it so fully in the belief of the sect. Its pulpit has been vocal with this teaching, and from its press has been issued many strong and convincing treatises on the subject. (3) If we carefully consider the widely varying tenets of Calvinism and Arminianism, it would scarcely be expected that the doctrine of Christian perfection should be accepted at all points and in perfect agreement by both these classes of Christians. Within the limits of one creed it would seem more reasonable to predicate possibilities of agreement, and that especially of the sect which had unfolded it so philosophically, and in the experience and lives of many of its members illustrated it so beautifully. (4) The Methodist denomination always has been, and to-day remains more scrupulously careful about her doctrines than the Church from which she sprang; and possibly quite as tenacious as any of the leading Protestant sects of the century. Yet it is noticeable that we have more discordant expressions on Christian perfection among us than on any other point of our belief. We would try, expel or silence a minister if he were half as divergent from our standards of faith on the subject of Justification, or the Lord's Supper, or baptism, or temperance, as many unblushingly avow themselves to be on Christian perfection. This theme has been so interwoven in our history from the beginning, and with such manifest advantage, that it should be our greatest glory.

We are in no haste to construe the prominence and encouragement which is apparently given to the opposition of Holiness. Those who truly represent Methodism on this vital

doctrine are consciously right, and are rapidly increasing.
Their prayer is for the Church, which as far as they can see,
is the hope of the world.

> " For her my tears shall fall;
> For her my prayers ascend;
> To her my cares and toils be given,
> Till toils and cares shall end."

On the other hand, the calm voice of history will persistently declare that when from within the denomination this
doctrine and experience was assailed by argument or innuendo;
or by its being placed in a light so false as to make it repel-
lent, the spiritual and temporal interest of the Church cor-
respondingly suffered.  In view of the future of Methodism,
for which the past Century gives such great promise, how
severe must be the denunciations of history against those who,
if successful, will have blighted these hopes, and deprived the
world of this aggregation of spiritual energy.

Isaac Taylor said that "foremost among the causes to which
may be attributed the unexampled success of the Wesleyan
body must be named its *unity* of *intention*, or adherence to,
and steady pursuit of a great principle," That master motive
of Methodism shines as plain as the sun in a cloudless sky;
and in successive editions of the Discipline it is affirmed of
the Methodists by her American Bishops, and by them quoted
from the Messrs. Wesleys themselves, that *" holiness was their
object.*  God then thrust them out to raise a holy people."
That they were thoroughly in earnest in this, appeared in
their hymns, their writings, their Church-work, their exhorta-
tions, their sermons, their lives, their deaths, and the results
which have followed.  The single conception which thrilled
their being was, "holiness, without which no man shall see the
Lord."  The single intention under which, with an unflagging
zeal, they pressed on, whether amid dangers, difficulties or

prosperity, was to lift all men into the utmost like-mindedness with Christ.   John Wesley repeatedly, variously, and without abatement, affirmed this to be the scope and intent of Methodism to the day of his death.   To get men converted, was but a part of his longing desire and arduous toil.   To have stopped there would have been more unwise than for the statesman to bend all his energies to increase the number of citizens, without any care as to developing in them the highest qualities of citizenship.   The friends of holiness in the Church "are not ambitious to enjoy its dignities, and administer its affairs;" but they could die, that it might constantly repeat, and exceed its best days of spiritual power; nor can they brook the thought that the wonders of grace our fathers beheld, are never again to be seen.   They cry day and night, O Lord, how long !

That there may be a clearer perception of the extent of the departures on this subject from the Methodistic view, look first at an authoritative statement of the doctrine.   The declarations and decisions of the early Annual Conferences in England, before the existence of the Legal Hundred, and prior to any delegated Conference, will be unquestioned authority.

Mr. Wesley records that "On Monday, the 25th of June, 1744, our first Conference began. * * * The next morning we seriously considered the doctrine of Sanctification or perfection."   "Our Second Conference began Aug. 1st, 1745. The next morning we spoke of Sanctification as follows:" here as at the first Conference the substance of the questions and answers are given.   "Our third Conference began Tuesday, May 26th, 1746.   In this we carefully read over the minutes of the two preceding Conferences to observe whether anything contained therein might be retrenched or altered on more mature consideration.   But we did not see cause to alter in any respect what we had agreed upon before.   Our fourth Confererence began on Tuesday, June 16th, 1747. As several persons were present who did not believe the doctrine of perfection, we agreed to examine it from the foundation." Then proceeds a full scriptural reply to the objections offered. If those who lay such stress on the non-profession of this grace by Wesley, and say they are imitating him, would only treat it as he did, how the word of the Lord would run and be glorified.

After speaking of publishing hymns (and quoting parts of them) in the years 1749 and 1752, in which Christian Perfection is clearly set forth, Mr. Wesley adds, " I have been the more large in these extracts, because hence it appears, beyond all possibility of exception, that to this day both my brother and I have maintained (1) That Christian Perfection is that love of God and our neighbor which implies deliverance from all sin. (2) That this is received merely by faith. (3) That it is given instantaneously in one moment. (4) That we are to expect it not at death but every moment: that now is the accepted time, now is the day of this salvation." Amplifying on the misconceptions in regard to this grace, and in the same connection, he affirms its nature, saying, "It is love governing the heart and life, and running through all our tempers, words, and actions." Again, he says, " Pure love reigning alone in the heart and life, this is the whole of Scriptural perfection." Almost immediately after, he says, "Not that 'to feel all love and no sin ' is a sufficient proof. Several have experienced this for a time before their souls were fully renewed. None therefore ought to believe that the work is done, till there is added the testimony of the Spirit, witnessing to entire sanctification as clearly as to justification." If we make this a fifth point, we have under Wesley's own hand and with the intent of setting it forth broadly to the Church, the formulated views of the very first Conferences of the Wesleyan Methodists, as

given in *A Plain Account of Christian Perfection.* Here it is:
(1) Christian Perfection is that love of God and our neighbor
which implies deliverance from all sin ; it is pure love reigning
alone in the heart and life. (2) This is received merely by
faith. (3) It is given instantaneously in one moment. (4)
We are to expect it not at death, but every moment, for now
is the accepted time, now is the day of this salvation. (5)
None ought to believe that this work is done till there is
added the testimony of the Spirit witnessing to entire sanctification as clearly as to justification.

Wesley and the early Methodists deemed this doctrine so
important that year after year in their Annual Conferences,
as soon as the routine business was dispatched, they immediately considered the subject of Christian Perfection, and
did not separate until all views were harmonized in its favor.
As in California, the presence of gold in larger or smaller
quantities could be found nearly everywhere from the Coast
Range of mountains to the loftiest peak of the Sierra Neva-
das, so all through the history and literature of Methodism,
from the experiences of believers bathed by the ocean of Perfect Love, up to the majestic Theological Institutes, sink a shaft
anywhere, and you will find the genuine article of Christian
Perfection. As long as history has a voice, no man can successfully controvert that Mr. Wesley believed it, preached it,
sung it, urged it, lived it, and with his compeers formulated
it in a logical system. The author of the most extreme attack
ever yet made upon this doctrine by a Methodist declares,
"The Methodist Church both in England and America hold
and have always held, the doctrine of Christian Perfection.
The Methodist Episcopal Church has never faltered in its
advocacy. Our Standard Theological works teach it, and
scarcely a year passes without some new publication on the
subject. (*Birthright of God's Children,* p. 13.) Yet this
author (p. 40) endeavors to make this doctrine unscriptural.

His language is, " Thus, little by little, the theory of a second distinct work grew up, and assumed what I cannot but regard, as an unscriptural form." Still on page 57 he styles it "a glorious doctrine." On page 42 he says " the mode of representing the doctrine became logically complete :" but on page 33 he affirms that Mr. Wesley's views were not well defined at the beginning, nor even at the end " * * * and that " they furnish no complete and consistent theory on the subject." He would account for the acceptance of the doctrine by the founder of Methodism in two ways, by adding thought to thought ; little by little, as logical necessity might urge him on. 2nd, Mr. Wesley's anxiety to explain his position, so as to accord with the latter part of the 9th Article of the Church of England, led him into manifold errors." p. 64. How much respect will be left for Mr. Wesley, if we can be persuaded that "this turbidness of the Wesleyan stream" resulted from his conscious preference of a fragment of an article of religion of the English Church over the Word of God ! If this author would cast doubt on the foundation of the doctrine because a thoroughly clear perception of it was not possessed at the outset, let it be remembered that thus it was with the Apostles ; the identical method they pursued in the acceptance of advanced positions in truth, Wesley pursued. He doubtless saw in their course, the Divine hand manifestly directing them. The record of the Word is too full and complete to leave any doubt as to their method. They made a careful comparison of the workings of the Holy Spirit on the hearts, and in the lives of men, with the teachings of God's Word. Their astonishment was aroused, their prejudices assaulted, and their pre-conceived theories overturned again and again ; but on they went wherever led by this conjoined Divine guidance. It was by precisely this method, prayerfully pursued through a series of years, that "the truth as it is in Jesus " of Perfect Love was formulated. Whoever heartily and prayerfully adopts the same method will soon, and in this life, enter upon,

> " A land of corn, and wine, and oil,
> Favour'd with God's peculiar smile,
>   With every blessing blest;
> There dwells the Lord our Righteousness,
> And keeps His own in perfect peace
>   And everlasting rest."

To recur to the question.

What are some of the principal differences of view?

It will be generally conceded that Methodists have constantly held that entire sanctification was necessarily subsequent to justification ; that inborn sin was not removed from the heart when the transgressions of the law of any individual life were pardoned.

Differing from this is the belief that the soul if freed from all inbred sin, or inherited corruption, at conversion, and hence that all subsequent lamentations of failure, are the cries of a heart backslidden from God—Such an uncharitable view of the Lord's heritage to us seems revolting.

A modified view of the same general position, is, that the soul at conversion is all that God would have it, and that whatever subsequent strivings and declinings we may have, only serve to reinstate us in the strength of our first love with the advantage of experience, to give steadiness and celerity to the movements of the Christian. This looks too much like continuance in sin for a season, that grace may abound.

Another modification still, is, also, antagonistic to any remaining depravity at conversion, and regards what has been generally accepted as evidences of pride, anger, and love of the world found in the heart of the believer, as *simply temptations* to pride, anger, and love of the world. These " evidences" are so sad and abundant, and so often result in the overt act that it would seem like trifling to call them *temptations.*

Another view is that the soul receives this grace by frequent installments continued through a series of years, and prior to death.—But why cannot God do it once?

Rather than one great blessing, it is more likely washing after washing of the purifying blood, say others.—"If by faith, why not now?"

It consists mainly in the modes of expression which different persons employ, or the same individuals under varying emotional influences, argue others.—The word of God solidly resists this.

It is a large blessing, but it must exert itself repressively, and never has power to extirpate sin from the soul say still others, who would be of great influence in our Zion.—" Reckon ye also yourselves to be indeed dead unto sin." So others in their zeal would faithfully warn against empyrean professions, too frequent introspection.—" Examine yourselves whether ye be in the faith."

But enough of this list. These are fair samples of the rest. We do not propose a full reply. All the principal objections may be classified as (1) those relating to the nature of the blessing, (2) those relating to the time of its reception, and (3) those which criticise the manner by which its professors may give their testimony of it. The first is now so much involved in the second ; and indeed those in the third, we believe, are not of very great moment in view of the decided importance of the second. So that our inquiry may resolve itself into this : Can Methodists be agreed as to the time when this blessing is received?

Surely there is no insuperable difficulties preventing Methodists from agreeing (1) that entire sanctification may take place at any moment, by faith, in the heart of one already justified.

All those Methodists who affirm sanctification as received

at the time of the soul's regeneration, are of the momentary faith, since they profess that in one moment they were justified. Why should they deny its momentary reception to those who are confident they did not receive it at conversion? 2. It is desirable and essential *that all* should have a grace "without which no man shall see the Lord." 3. If the many who *know they did not receive entire sanctification* at the time of their justification, may have it by faith in one moment, to grant a thus would be more to the Divine glory, our good, and through us to the good of others, than to receive it in installments spread over a series of years, since life is crowded so full of uncertainties. 4. The most marvelous demonstration of the *uniformity of law*, exists in every department of God's work. In the same realm or department, He never works in variable ways; or to accomplish His purpose in a single direction, changes His plan at different times. Any seeming change is provided for and included in the original place. The constituent parts of water now, are what they were when the crystal drops gushed forth from the creative fountain. Faith is now no more a pre-requisite of salvation than it was with the first sinner. Though the evidence, or the witness of the Divine forgiveness may have dawned its force upon us, increasing until the sun of this favor was fully orbed, the process of our forgiveness in God's mind was as instantaneous as the lightning's flash. So in this mind, the law of uniformity would teach us, it must be with our sanctification. Joseph Cook, who is so profoundly stirring the Anglo Saxon intellect, says in his lecture on "Conscience as the foundation of the religion of Science," "Forever and forever we must acknowledge the unity and universality of the law."

To reach these conclusions would not seem difficult to one well disposed towards making the effort.

Dr. Bushnell's description of the effects of receiving this grace is clear." All the mixed causes involved in sin or spirit-

ual impurity will fall into chime, and all the foul currents of
evil suggestion be cleared to a transparent flow. The mind
will grow regular and simple in its action, ceasing to be vexed,
as it was by noxious mixtures of fear, selfishness, doubt and
temptation." He declares it is not difficult to realize this
" when you have it as the accepted aim and effort of your
life to be assimilated in purity to God; for when such a desire becomes practically fixed in you, the way will certainly
be found. The way to purity is difficult of discovery to those
who practically do not care for it."

Here lies the whole gist of this subject. Does any soul
really long for it, then the way will certainly be found.

Joseph Cook says, "It should be asserted by science in the
name of experiment that man may become a partaker of the
Divine nature." Again, "Repetition of experiment! That
is the scientific test of deepest significance. Religious science
does not flinch in the application of it. In that test she finds
all her victories. * * I assert that it is a fixed natural law
that when you yield utterly to God He streams into you, gives
a new sense of His presence, and imparts a strength unknown
before. Will you try such self-surrender, and then will you
repeat the experiment as opportunity offers? I care not how
often. * * I affirm that in these billions of opportunities for
experiments, in these ten thousand times ten thousand chances
to test whether I am right or wrong, you will not find one
chance failing to give you this verdict, that if you yield utterly to God, He will stream through you." Joseph Cook's
lecture, " Conscience as the foundation of the religion of
Science." In another lecture he declares, " It is a right heart
that in the end makes a safe head." Repeat your experiment
in the case of a recently but soundly converted soul ten thousand times, and get such men as John Wesley, Adam Clarke,
Joseph Benson, Francis Asbury, Wilbur Fisk, Stephen Olin,
or Nathan Bangs to examine them, and they do not find one

who bears the marks of a co-etaneous justification and entire sanctification, though they may find, in increasing numbers, those who have received the latter grace soon after the former. Reverse the test, and by hundreds of thousands the witnesses declare that though they have received pardon, they never knew the grace of perfect love. Can any contrary theory soever have the hardihood to hope for acceptance in the face of these ten thousand times repeated tests? God changes not, therefore these results are changeless. The theorists must conform to the facts, since they cannot annihilate or change them.

A contributor on the editorial page of *Christian Advocate* for Dec. 27, 1877, makes this broad, true, but sad statement, "No doctrine of Methodism has been so much tampered with as the sanctification of the believer." When the venerable Alfred Brunson, D. D., applied to the General Conference of 1872 for a revision, or restatement, of the doctrines of the Methodist Episcopal Church, accompanied with a carefully prepared exhibit of doctrines, that conference referred the matter to the Committee on Revisals. After some consideration, this Committee desired its reference to the Bishops with a request that they should report on the same at the General Conference of 1876.

By a very full vote, the paper was passed over to our Chief Shepherds, who by their position, and acquaintance with the history and workings of the Church, were so well qualified to express an authoritative opinion. At the ensuing General Conference the Bishops made their report, and we submit the rule itself, upon which the report was based, and a few extracts of that report, upon the change of the rule. It should be borne in mind that if the power to alter the doctrines of the Church exists anywhere, it could exist nowhere but in the General Conference. That body is especially prohibited from making such change by the constitution of the Church.

1st Restrictive Rule. "The General Conference shall no revoke, alter, or change our Articles of Religion, nor establish any new standards or rules of doctrine contrary to our present existing and established standards of doctrine." (*Methodist Discipline*. There are six of these Restrictive Rules. In the last of these, by a method there definitely pointed out, it is provided "to alter any of the above restrictions, excepting the first article." So that by the lawful method designated, the Church *could* "do away the Episcopacy;" "or destroy the plan of our itinerant general superintendency;" "revoke or change the General Rules of Society," or "do away the privilege" of "trial by Committee" of ministers and members; but never, no never, to "alter" "our present existing and established standards of doctrine." We can readily trace from the sons to their fathers in the Church, the profound and rightful regard had for the Episcopacy, its itinerant Superintendency, and the other institutions embraced in the Restrictive Rules; but as much deeper than this as is the fathomless ocean below the swallows of the brooklet, was their unalterable devotion to the doctrines of the Church, as the basis of fundamental saving truth.

In their report with reference to the change, or re-statement of doctrine, the Bishops say: "The right of the General Conference to act in the premises is involved. If such power is implied, it is found only by a questionable inference. * * The framers of the Constitution did not intend that any alterations should be made in the Articles of Religion, and did intend that alterations should not be made. * * The manifest purpose of the framers of the Constitution was that the established doctrines of the Church should be forever safe from alteration."—*General Conference Journal* of 1876. Hence they unanimously reported against revision, and their view was very fully affirmed by vote of the General Conference. Why then is the doctrine of "the sanctificaticn of the believer" "tampered with" more than any other doctrine of Methodism? And why from so many turrets and towers of the Church is this opposition flag thrown to the breeze? From the loyal side of the denomination we are glad to say to these tamperers "your endeavors are all in vain, for the established doctrines of the Church are forever safe from alteration."

If our doctrines, as declared by the framers of the Constitution of our Church, and the construction put on their purpose by the Bishops and General Conference, make our doctrines unalterable, what course should be pursued? 1. We say we want no new standard; no revision of doctrine, and no abatement of zeal to press the truth in any direction, for one truth never collides with another; they run in heavenly parallel grooves, and are always mutually promotive of each other. 2. Let the official press of the Church, and its pulpit, hold their utterances on entire sanctification as carefully to the authorized Catechism and standards of our faith, as they do scrupulously revere our denominational views on other important doctrines. Do not discriminate unfavorably among them, but tenaciously hold to them all. Where does any Methodist get his right or authority to do otherwise? 3. Let those who have, by the suffrage of the Church, been entrusted to high position, be as careful to speak or print with as much concern for the conservation of Perfect Love, as they do of the other vital doctrines of the Church: and as occasion may demand, reprove and rebuke those who may do otherwise. As heartily avoid all innuendoes towards, and the travestying of this truth, as of any other truth. Is not this reasonable? In short, be loyal Methodists in this respect, as well as in all others, and reconciliation in sentiment may be confidently expected. It must not be forgotten that Mr. Wesley gave very great prominence to the subject of entire sanctification, but we ask the modest right that it be treated and greeted with as much affection and regard as is paid to any other doctrine.

To sum up our views:

1. No doctrine of our Church has been formulated more carefully and accepted more fully, by Wesley and his compeers, at the early Conferences, and subsequently, than the doctrine of Entire Sanctification.

2. These fathers of the Church frequently urged upon ministers and people to make this truth very prominent in preaching and experience.

3. By the act of Methodism throughout its whole history entire sanctification is as clearly a standard doctrine with the denomination as is that of justification by faith, or any other doctrine soever.

4. Mr. Wesley put in the frame-work of the itinerancy the strongest barriers against diversity of view and teaching on this subject. This was done by refusing a voice and vote in Annual Conference action, and afterward, in General Conference representation, to those who could not answer "Yes" to the questions, "Are you going on to perfection?" "Do you expect to be made perfect in love in this life?" "Are you groaning after it?"

5. The most solemn obligation rests upon every minister in full connexion in the Methodist Church, to enter upon and experimentally enjoy the blessing of Perfect Love.

6. No member of the Church, in high or humble position, has any more right to "tamper" with or ignore this doctrine, than any other received doctrine of the Church.

7. As our standard doctrines, by the constitution of the Church, the decision of the Bishops, and the General Conference, are unalterable, everything said or written by members of the denomination against Perfect Love, is a wilful disturbance of the peace of the Church; and the humblest member in the fold may and should protest against such course by whomsoever pursued.

8. Since this doctrine has been made prominent by the

fathers and framers of the Church, it is as great a mistake and wrong to cast reflections and innuendoes upon its sincere professors as upon the sincere professors of justification.

9. Liberty of speech, without the Church, is the right of all; but that liberty of speech which destroys the very foundations of the Church, is the right of none, while within the fold.

10. Disagreements are more the outgrowth of the head than the heart; therefore a prayerful search for light and grace; a complete surrender of the entire being to God; and the taking hold of the Divine promises by faith, would bring every one making the honest effort into the fullest accord; and the Church under God, to be the foremost factor in the evangelization of the world.

11. Disagreements on this doctrine, should be honestly impossible within the pales of the denomination.

12. To press this truth, and its experience, with all the heavenly persuasives of which we may be possessed, is the foretold Wesleyan method of making the Church the most potential possible during the second century of her history.

*The need of agreement.*

In disagreement there is a possibility of partisan feeling, and strong expression which is liable to a harsh construction. Too much time and strength may be given to strife, which will not promote the Divine glory. We may thus provoke each other to animosity rather than to good works. But if possible a still more important reason for an agreement upon the basis of the truth is found in the fact of the achievements of the Gospel as already effected.

There is no room to doubt but that, in Christian countries, community at large has decidedly higher and clearer moral conceptions, and that the general conduct of the average non-professor, is much improved over what it was in less favored times. General sentiment now, will not endure the semi-barbaric practices as once they were permitted ; if not sanctioned, especially when directed against out-spoken Christians. However others may explain this wonderful improvement of the manners and views of community, the lovers of the Lord are warranted in affirming this change is the result of the leavening and uplifting power of the gospel. So far has this gone that the average man of the world appears to about as good advantage as the average Christian. Society has been so toned up by the inculcations of religious truth, that the Church and the world, in some aspects of the case are not a little like each other. Many a candid observer of this is withheld from seeking a new heart, as he asks, "What is the difference?" It may be affirmed, also, that as the distinctive lines are effaced, you have the development of a two-fold tendency, viz., the world, in its external deportment, becoming more like that of the Church, and of the Church conforming to the world.

Growing out of this state of things it becomes of momentous importance that the disparity between the unsaved world and the Christian world shall be as broad and deep as ever it was, if not in outward deportment then certainly and indispensably in communion with God, and like-mindedness with Christ. The Church may rejoice that the world has been brought so far forward. Yet this shall not be so great a cause of congratulation if the Church has not the requisite spiritual power to lead the world to an inward possession of divine grace. The voice of Church history is pronounced, that only by the infusion of all the mind which was in Christ, can the Church be kept decidedly in the advance. Exhortation, praying, preaching on the ordinary plane of religious life, or the diffusion of Christian literature, does not, has not, and presumably never will keep the Church from degenerating into a very perceptible conformity to the world, dead at heart, if it be but well habited, well surrounded, and well behaved. If the Church is to be continuously the "salt of the earth," she must "be filled with the Spirit," and to "overcome" at every point and always, she must "put on the whole armor of God." No denomination, born of whatsoever intensity of fervor and spirituality, can withstand the paralyzing influences of an insidious growth of worldliness within its own bosom, an indifference to an experimental acquaintance of heart purity is sure to follow. The grave of ritualism, formalism, or scepticism, is certain to receive all that is vital to godliness of such a Church. Revivals of religion can operate not to prevent but merely retard this sad result; for the revivalistic spirit will in turn be smitten with the fatal paralysis. It may take longer or shorter time, according to the spiritual resistance, but the end is inevitable.

In all this we say nothing of the organic body. Like the Yew tree, organic Church life may thrive in the midst of death. Our position is that the ultimate spiritual life and power of the Church depends not at all on vast proportions and rapid accumulation of members, but solely and forever on the faithful performance of that command which Jesus emphasized as He did no other: "Thou shalt love the Lord thy God with all thy heart, and with all thy soul, and with all thy mind. This is the first and great commandment. And the second is like unto it, Thou shalt love thy neighbor as thyself. On these two commandments hang all the law and the prophets."

With such authority we have no apology for desiring perfect agreement within the Church of our choice, for a Baptist with more propriety might discourage immersion within his denomination, than that a Methodist should darken counsel about entire sanctification.

May God give this cause such help that it may never know an ebb.

Thursday evening, after a powerful testimony and consecration meeting led by Sister Inskip, Bro. John Parker read a paper on

## HOLINESS AS RELATED TO THE CONVERSION OF THE WORLD.

Matthew 5 : 16, also Isaiah 60: 1-5, 19-22.

### REV. JOHN PARKER.

You may regard the portions of Scripture I have read as a text suggesting two thoughts in the direction of which I propose to speak.

I. The godly shining that carries conviction.

II. And the conviction that will lead men to Christ.

The shining demanded by the text is the outward revealing of the inward life. There will be no outward shining without inward, spiritual light and life. This demand for a shining life puts the subject entirely beyond all pretence and seeming; it is a divine call for the genuine, for only the genuine shines; and only a shining life carries conviction. The moonlit light obscured by drifting clouds is a mixed and dim shining, a struggle for the mastery between light and darkness. You have seen also the ghastly glimmer of the phosphorescence emitted by decay. Neither of these symbolize the shining life; they neither suggest warmth nor attraction. It is the demand of your Master in the text that the light you are to shed shall have a charm and a divine warmth, for it is to attract and fix the love of those who never loved God, and have no knowledge of, or relish for His favor or communion.

This shining, attracting life is also to reveal in you the existence of pure, holy, divine character, where conscience holds dominion, and honor and righteousness are esteemed as essential to your life as the blood in your veins. These are to be the perpetual outshining of the divine enthronement within your heart. Teaching the fact, that in one man at least God has restored the splendors of His own dwelling, and rekindled the fire of His love, that from this nature, once so sordid and sinful, He has expelled the dominion of self and now His Spirit fills all your life with the ministries of love.

Thus the first text is a *divine demand, and is peculiarly individual in its application.* " Let *your* light shine," &c.

The second portion of Scripture I read is God's promise to His shining Church of all she needs for the fulfilment of her mission in carrying salvation to all the world. Light is the thing most needed in darkness, and the mission of God's Church is to a world full of darkness and ignorance and alienation from God.

In such a world the Church needs light and vital heat more than anything else. Light to reveal her angel character, and divine errand, and to give to the world the evidence that with her is God's abiding glory. That He is in the midst of her people, living in their life, and sanctifying by His gracious communion. So has He made His Church the light-bringer for this night-mantled world, and set against its gross darkness and desolation the light and glory of His shining Church. This second text I read is, as if it said: "It is morning at last." Arise and shine, the night has been long, and darkness dense and deep has covered the earth, but now God will put Himself and His shining Church against all this darkness, and ignorance and crime, and they shall flee away. His glory shining through the channel of His sanctified Church shall herald and bring a bright, broad day of universal light. Even the besotted condition of the Gentiles, as seen by the prophet, shall offer no effectual barrier to resist the attraction which shall attend His Church. And to the Church's shining and healing power all nations shall flow and run together.

*Shining for God is holiness,* for holiness is love speaking, and acting and sacrificing self, and bearing burdens and sharing reproach for the glory of God and the salvation of men.

There is a technical and an evangelical definition of holiness. The technical is that which makes it represent the whole theory of faith and life of perfect love, or entire sanctification. The evangelical sense of the term, and that to which I shall call your attention, is, that holiness is the life, the outshining of a sanctified nature. The efficacy of a doctrine is in the life it produces. If that life is more divine, and more divinely human, more loving, and therefore more unselfish, more gentle and pure and believing than it was in its regenerate or mixed condition, then it bears the divine imprint of holiness, and God has need of it and work for it to do in leading the world back to Himself. *This is the shining which carries conviction.* There are some things God cannot do. He cannot approve that which is contrary to His own nature. He cannot love unholiness. He cannot bestow such a power of convincing energy on a backslidden Church or individual, as that men in sin will be likely to fall in love with Christ through its influence. I do not intend by the definition given to divorce the theory of holiness from the life; I believe there is much of the life of holiness in the world that is not related to the profession or teaching of the theory, and much theory that is not related to the life. I believe that a consecrated heart and life, brimming with love to God and man, full of all goodness and gentleness and truth, a life of self-denial and Christ-exalted, hating sin, and working in purity and faith and divine fellowship, is holiness, called by whatever name. And this is that winsome piety, which having power with God, is related to the conversion of the world. *Holy living then as related to the world's conversion* is the subject of the text, and the thought I wish to impress on your minds.

Is it so related, as cause and effect are related? Does the world's conversion depend in any important sense on the ho-

liness of the Church and its individual members? I have
shown you God's answer to this question in the verses I read,
which answer is, substantially, "make the Church what I
would have her to be, let her realize my ideal of saintly character, fill all her life with the light and warmth of holiness,
then make her to the world all she is capable of being and doing and the world will be speedily converted."

God answered this question also with wonderful emphasis
at the beginning of the Church's history in her Christian form.
The Saviour had completed His atoning work, organized the
agencies of His Church, established its ceremonial and sacraments, now He will emblazon on His Church's banner her
new symbol. In the rending of the veil the symbols of the
old dispensation had passed away. Altar and incense, urim
and thummim, breastplate and candlestick, these had kept
alive through ages dark and barbarous, the faith and hope of
the Church, while that Church had been chiefly limited to a
single nationality. Now the Gentiles are to come to its light,
the whole earth is to see the salvation of God. The old symbol-
ism is abolished, as insufficient. A new symbol shall indicate to
the Church the source of her power, and the certainty of her
triumph; it shall be tongues of fire. Speech on fire, the
speech human, the fire divine. Everywhere the burning
tongue speaking of a positive personal experience of salvation,
speaking because of profound convictions of the truth and
availableness of the gospel, and this speech set on fire by the
Holy Ghost,—to melt and thaw the winter of unbelief, and
indifference, and turn it into the summer of a personal, perpetual, gladness and beauty and life.

But the symbol is only a suggestion, a sign; and useless
except as a channel of the thing signified, which, in this case,
was to be hearts all ablaze with the divine baptism. Even
this divine symbol, without the divine fire, is only like the
glittering armor of a dead warrior with the warrior buried,

or like a painted dinner on a painted plate to a starving man. And yet this divine ideal of the Church's power, as indicated at the Pentecost, is still a cherished picture to the visible Church; and hung up in the gallery of her great admiration, her pulpits love to talk about it, and her people to sing of it; *but where is the fire?* Where the holy separated Church of the Lord Jesus cleansed from sin, emptied of selfishness and fire-crowned with tongues of flame? I do not expect answer from any apostate branches of the visible Church, but I ask it, with deep solicitude, of that part of the visible Church, which, holding to the fundamental doctrines of Evangelical godliness love to point us to the Pentecost as the beginning of their history and the promise of their ultimate success. The Church of a sound orthodoxy, but a mixed experience and a compromising life. Whose attitude toward worldliness should be protest, but is too commonly imitation. I ask of her, *where is the fire?* Ye have your altars, and your service, and your costly surroundings and suggestions of worship, but *where is the fire?* Your ranks are chiefly kept from depletion and utter waste by the slow processes of Sabbath-school labor, a kind of generative Christianity. Ye have played at Christianity through generations of mixed life and experience, and have dreamed and sung of a world conquered, then have died, and the refrain has been taken up by another generation; thus ye have flattered yourselves and each other with untroubled security, regarding the world's conversion. Whereas the merest rim of the world has yet been reached and won for Christ. With fourteen hundred million dwellers on the earth to-day, it is doubtful if fifty millions—or one in twenty-eight —know anything of saving godliness. Where, then, is your mighty power of Christian proselytism that should enter the dark frowning lines of heathenism and Romanism and infidelity and indifference, and, realizing prophetic expectation, capture the world for Christ. If it be true that your

Church machinery and your mixed life are all the arrangements God has intended, then why are ye yet on the defensive? Why look on appalled at the spectacle of a world
that lieth in the wicked one, having little hope or expectation
that ye can speedily win the world to the love and obedience
of Christ? Why expend all your force in taking care of yourselves, and keeping your numbers from depletion? I went
to the excellent meeting, at Dr. Palmer's, last week. As I
entered, the meeting had begun. I heard the devout and
happy throng shouting peans of victory, as if the long dream of
the Church had become reality. One shouted, "New York
for Jesus." Another responded, "Brooklyn for Jesus." Another shouted "Newark for Jesus." I closed my eyes, and
instantly I had a vision. I saw the devil laughing at this
chosen company of God's people ; for had he not one of the
leading pastors of the city writing weekly articles for the *New
York Ledger*, and the *New York Ledger* in turn giving immense sums to build and support a palace-church to flatter
the vanity of this minister? Another leading pastor of this
city, wishing the city full of beer-shops as a cure for drunken-
ness. While other leading pastors were chiefly occupied in
the religion of millinery and gowns, and cassocks, and
splendid architecture, and gorgeous costly ceremonial and
display, other leading pastors were devising methods in coun-
cil, to drive from his flock a godly shepherd, whose only
crime was holy living, holy teaching and obedience to the Holy
Ghost, while two-thirds of the remaining pastors in these cities
are tied hand and foot to the mill of Church debts, grinding out
energy and heart to save what semblance of Christianity, we
have, from the sheriff's sale. And all this, in the great centres
of Christian influence and enterprise, while the bulk of
Christian laymen spend more money in tobacco than they do
for Christ and the world's conversion. The world converted
forsooth. Alas! alas! As the vision ended, I asked again,

9

*where is the fire?* In asking this question, my heart would die in hopelessness, did I not believe that the divine fire is as available to the Church of God to-day as when it crowned the early Church, and this fire-baptism is the holiness that is to convert the world. Sin burnt out, and purity, and righteousness, and truth, and love, and goodness, and self-forgetfulness burnt in. With this, altar and pulpit, and pew; tongue, and heart, and life, will be on fire. Then the world will be attracted, convicted, converted. Till then, God can neither use nor trust His Church to do this work. Many have been saved, many will be saved in spite of her worldliness and her mixed life, for God will honor His truth and save men wherever its essentials are preached. Thus far what I have said relates to the conversion of the world through the instrumentality of a holy, witnessing Church. This will suggest

II. *The conviction that leads men to Christ.*—"Let your light so shine before men," etc. This is God's process of converting the world. Holy men shining to win others, these in turn repeating the process, this process multiplied, and the world is speedily converted. So that the personal holiness that carries conviction, by the charm of its shining and the strength and consistency of its character and life, is vitally related to the world's conversion.

Presuming that you believe that the conversion of the world is according to the divine plan and purpose, let me further suggest in what way the doctrine and experience of Christian holiness is related to it.

1st. Holiness is the opposite of selfishness, and selfishness is the most formidable antagonist to the salvation of the world. Holiness is the life of perfect love, and perfect love is made glad by every new demand which God makes upon it for sacrifice or service. This restores to the Church the doctrine and practice of Christian stewardship,—God's absolute ownership of everything you have, or can be, or do. This removes financial embarrassment from the Church, making the world's wealth available for the world's conversion. This makes unnecessary all doubtful methods of raising money for the work of the Church, holding the Church and each believer answerable to the divine call for service, sacrifice, or death. This restores the days of heroic faith and daring for God, the days of a self-denying ministry and a consecrated Church. Thus far we have seen how a holy man and a holy Church is God's ideal instrument for the conversion of the world. And He has made no other arrangements. We know not, that He ever will. He has promised to gird with all needed power, and supply with all needed resources such a man, and such a Church. Thus linked with the resources and destiny of His Church, she becomes omnipotent. In such a union, the question of her triumph and the world's conversion is answered. If a man in financial enterprise is as strong as his backers, a holy Church is strong as the available and used power which God offers to her help. God says to the Church, "If thou arise and shine, thy light being come and the glory of the Lord risen upon thee, thy sun shall no more go down, neither shall thy moon withdraw itself, for the Lord shall be thine everlasting light, and the days of thy mourning shall be ended. Thy people also shall be all righteous, they shall inherit the land forever, the branch of my planting, the work of my hands, that I may be glorified. A little one shall become a thousand, and a small one a strong nation. I, the Lord, will hasten it." In these and kindred words, God relates His "shalls," and your speedy and universal triumph, with your obedience and your shining.

There are three things which determine the measure of influence which holiness in a believer exerts upon others.

*First.* Does it manifestly satisfy his own soul? Is this evident to all about him? Has he spiritual rest and power? Does he evidently put the past under the atoning blood and let it stay there? Does he put the present and future into the divine care and disposal, so that his temper is sweetened and his soul untroubled about possibilities? Is he so satisfied in God that he does not wish to supplement his divine communion with worldly fellowships and pleasures? Is the forbidding that he " be not conformed to this world," irksome or agreeable?

*Second.* Is he grounded in granite honesty and sincerity, " commending himself to every man's conscience in the sight of God " in all honesty and godly sincerity? Is the divine favor a priceless treasure, and is Christian influence more valuable to him than gold? Do men feel that he can be trusted anywhere?

*Third.* Is his zeal controlled and tempered by godly wisdom, loving, steady, strong and consistent? For I am sure this Convention is not in sympathy with a mere emotional holiness, a religion of the sensibilities which expends itself in the intoxication of religious enthusiasm. We contend for, and will be satisfied with nothing less than all the inward cleansing, the perfection of love, the power of a conscience cleansed by the blood and restored to dominion in the life, the absolute separation unto God, and the recognition of the doctrine of personal ownership, responsibility and communion with God. The light, the life, the victory and the assurance of hope that is promised to those who have fellowship with the Father. With life, property and service ever available at the call of your divine Master. This is holiness, this is that salt of Heaven which put anywhere in unobstructed relation to this corrupted earth, will heal and save it.

In the recent pastoral address of the Bishops of the Methodist Episcopal Church, is one of the saddest exhibitions of a great Church halting at the threshold of possibility. Halting and shrinking because of unconsecrated wealth and perverted self-love. They tell us that " neither financial embarrassment, nor want of means can account for the crippled condition of our great work ; that luxuries and extravagances among our people are as conspicuous as ever.'' If this fact is so deplorable, why did they not use their great opportunity at the ear of the Church in telling her that a restoration of original Methodist success requires a restoration of the old heroic self-denying consecrated spirit of holiness? Why not reiterate the old Wesleyan teaching, that a revival of holiness in doctrine, life and experience would so quicken the conscience of the Church, so restore the deep sense of personal responsibility, and so reanimate the old spirit of our fathers, that, expecting great things from God, they would attempt great things for God. I desire to speak with reverence of our chief pastors, but it seems to me that they see an evil they dare not assail, and a remedy they fear to insist upon. The evil is the indifference of the Church to the old Wesleyan doctrine of entire sanctification, the remedy its immediate restoration to our pulpits and experience.

It has been charged against the doctrine of Christian holiness, as advocated by the friends of this Convention, that it relates chiefly to the sensibilities. Rev. C. G. Finney, in his recently published life, makes this the reason why he could not accept the teaching of Methodism on this subject. If that is true of our advocacy—and it is worth while to hearken to the suggestions of so holy and sagacious a man as Mr. Finney ; if this is true, then we are yet a very weak people, and but poorly adapted to the work of converting the world. If holiness among us is simply a thing of excitement, and occasional spurts of enthusiastic and joyful testimony, if it has not subdued and sanctified the heart, if it has not restored the conscience to purity and dominion, if we are yet selfish and self-asserting as against the claims of God upon all we have and are, and if the tendency of our teaching and our literature on this subject is rather to quicken emotions than to holy living, then let us be thankful that Mr. Finney has pointed out our mistake. But is it so? I think not. It is true that we have given prominence to New Testament teaching as to the duty of sanctified believers to be happy and to publish their joy, and this is the will of God concerning them, but it is also true that we insist in all our teaching on holy living in all godliness and sincerity and truth. On an immediate surrender of everything to God, and acknowledgment of the Divine ownership of all we have. We do everywhere insist on the necessity of hearts consciously purified, and lives unworldly and wholly consecrated. This admitted, and we yet contend that it is the will of God that believers rejoice evermore.

It is said again that the friends of the doctrine of holiness are so much occupied with the matter of their own experience, they have little time or disposition to save men from their sins and lead them to Christ. A comparison in zeal and self-denying work for the salvation of souls, between the friends of the doctrine of holiness and those who are not avowedly its advocates — might be made, I think, to the advantage of the former. I believe the facts are so palpable that no unprejudiced mind will attempt to dispute the matter. I am satisfied that the average labors of the friends of holiness result in the conversion of far greater numbers—than the equal labors of those who are not recognized as the advocates of perfect love, by faith, now, and that the most successful evangelists and pastors are those who are interested in holiness as a specialty. But this does not answer the objection. Is it true that we are occupied too much with introspection and analysis of our personal religious condition? If it is true we ought to know it, and be humble enough to confess it. I believe there is much truth in the objection, and that just here is our weakness. At the holiness meeting to which I have referred, a meeting composed of the very elect of this and adjoining cities, I made this matter a special study. It was a meeting of unusual interest and power. And yet, except by one or two persons, not a word was said about the salvation of sinners; and what was said was incidental. The meeting was very rich in facts relating to personal inquest, personal discovery, and personal triumph, but the unsaved world was nearly forgotten. Holiness is so related to the salvation of the world, that it must take it into its deepest solicitude and largest plans and efforts, and hold it there.

Allow me to say, that I think I see where the friends of holiness unwittingly obstruct its progress, and thereby hinder the conversion of the world.

*First. By their Severity.* Holiness is lovely. Its profession and enjoyment must be lovely, or God cannot use it for the world's conversion. He promises that sorrow and sighing shall flee away before the march of His returning and triumphant Church,—on whose head is joy and gladness. Fair as the moon, bright as the sun, yet terrible as a bannered army.

*Second.* Do we not hinder the work by our want of that godly wisdom which wins confidence, and that manifest persistency and singleness of purpose that compels the conviction of our absolute consecration? We are not only to shine,— but to "*so shine,*" etc. Astronomers can tell us the heat of a planet by its distance from the sun, so men know your distance from the cross by the influence it exerts, and the steadiness with which it holds you. Holy men should always remember that their life terminates not in themselves. You are to "walk worthy of the Lord unto all pleasing—being fruitful in every good work." To "walk in wisdom toward them that are without." Your fitness or otherwise, as an instrument for the world's conversion, depends on the abiding baptism of the Holy Spirit in your life; also, on the abiding impression you make on the minds of men, as to where your love centres.—"Does he dwell in God?"

Holiness should relate you to the world's conversion by

simplifying your aims and concentrating your energies on the one supreme law of the believer's life, *the glory of God.* Doing everything for His glory, you brush aside all other rules of conduct and life. Preference and prejudice, and taste and bondage to usage, and fear of criticism, all are gone as rules of life. Cowardice gives way to courage, and policy to supreme principle.

Holiness endears to its friends the word of God in its utmost demands, as well as in its fullness of promise. In making the heart clean, God brings the life into pleasant harmony with His "statutes and judgments." Whatever the tendency in our treatment of this doctrine to lead and leave the Church too much in the realm of the emotional, it cannot be said that the advocates of holiness are not upright in their dealings. Has any one heard of a single professor of the experience of holiness who is guilty of defalcation or the fraudulent use of entrusted property? And this is no small matter in view of the facts that are constantly coming to light. For the world loathes religious pretence without religious principle. Holiness is not the mere impulse of the hour, but is the abiding purpose and daily life of the soul. It is rock honesty and sincerity everywhere, that no opportunity can beguile, and no price can purchase. Thus the personality which holiness creates, and the stewardship which holiness restores, and the glad service which holiness commands relates it vitally to the conversion of the world.

The conditions of successful effort then, for the world's conversion, are:

1st. A strong and abiding conviction in the Church, of the perishing condition of the race without the gospel, and of the absolute impossibility of salvation, through any human system of recovery whether of culture or self-restraint or development.

2d. Also a profound conviction that the gospel is God's

only arrangement for the salvation of a lost world. That this divine arrangement is available to all, and is suited to all, and is fitted to heal and sanctify fully, the entire heart and soul of every one coming to it for salvation, by restoring to such, a personal consciousness of pardon, divine communion and cleansing through the atonement. And in order that God's provision may be put where the necessity is so deeply felt, the person sending it must be so redeemed from selfishness as that he shall make the perishing condition of the race and the honor of God, the sole reason for his enterprise.

The person carrying it, the preacher, teacher, or missionary, must love his neighbor, namely, all mankind, irrespective of color or distance. And love for God and his neighbor must be so palpable and controlling as to induce a persistency of effort, not to be discouraged by failures, or delays, or the follies of others. He must be so related to God by faith in Him, as that God can make him an unobstructed channel of light and power for the elevation and restoration of men to Himself. This believer can be, must be, holy by a positive cleansing from all sin, and vitalized and inspired by constant living contact with God.

Thus living he will readily believe, thus believing he will pray, thus praying he will expect, thus expecting he will work, thus working he will win. Multiply this man, and his praying, believing, working power by the number of believers on the earth, and the world will be speedily converted to God.

*Finally.* It is of the very nature of holiness to be aggressive in its efforts, and those who labor to promote it, and to seek the salvation of men by becoming zeal and self-denial, must antagonize ease and selfishness, and the worldly spirit in the Church, wherever found. This will provoke opposition. The strong and wealthy ecclesiasticism of his day antagonized and killed our Master. It will not be friendly to you, in so far as you are perfect, you shall be as your Master. He therefore, who is not willing to pay the price, had better stand back from the aggressive efforts of holiness, until he receives the baptism of power. For holiness is sure to be a costly investment at present; but a profitable one not far hence. Our cause and its certain triumph must not be judged by the esteem or favor which men give it, but by the word of God. In the history of Gideon and his little band of water-lappers, God taught us that seen strength and resources may be few and feeble, but linked with the unseen, they are infinite and must prevail.

What then is our immediate duty and necessity as the friends and advocates of the doctrine and experience of scriptural holiness?

1st. An immediate and complete surrender of all the possessions and possibilities of our life, to be sanctified, sealed and made available for the Divine call and work. Ready as stewards for any trust, as servants for any labor, as a sacrifice for any altar. A light in this world and a guide to a better.

2d. A definite, courageous avowal of a possibility of a personal experience of perfect love, so definite as to be easily and always understood. And this personal holiness to be set forth by us, not as the accidental and occasional issue of a severe struggle, but as the great end of the atonement, with a patient persistency that cannot be hindered or turned aside by any degree of hostility or indifference. Hold the light up so high, and walk in it yourself, so clearly, that honest conscientious believers, who are seeking the light, may obtain it, and the ungodly may regard you as chosen channels of Divine grace and power.

3. A manifest loyalty to the word and will of God as revealing His pleasure concerning our spiritual and consecrated life. Let the unlikeness of the true Church of God, and of the best average conditions of the world be seen to be this, our unmistakable communion with God, and our extreme sensitiveness to the perilous condition of the unsaved.

Let us silence the complaining of any who mistakenly say of us, that we are exclusive and exacting, and that we are not becomingly concerned for the salvation of the perishing, by our earnest, patient toil to save the unsaved. Let us believe and act upon the fact that this doctrine and experience promoted by preaching, or testimony, or holiness literature does wonderfully vitalize the Church, and will surely hasten the time predicted in the text. Let us do all we can by teaching, testimony and example to send men to their Bibles and their knees to seek this cleansing grace. A clear personal enjoyment and freshness of unction in this grace is very important for the glow, and warmth, and strength, and gladness of our own hearts. But we shall fail to relate as we ought, this subject to the salvation of the world, unless it be seen that our chief concern is the salvation of perishing men. Saved ourselves and everything surrendered to God, once for all, our daily solicitude should be seen to be the bringing of men to Christ for salvation. The friends of holiness will do little to convert the world, if like the boy, who planted a peach-tree and took it up each week to see if the roots were growing, they return all the while to an examination of their frames and feelings. God is willing to give us all the strength and liberty, and love, and rest, and power He has promised to His chosen ones, but He wants it all made serviceable in His kingdom as lifting power. While Jesus was in an agony for a lost world, the disciples slept. Let us be warned by their example and inspired by His. Sympathy with the world's morally desolate and lost condition, and a yearning compassion like His to save it, is Holiness in its Divinest form and fruitfulness and this is related to the world's conversion.

This essay came like a message from God to the people; and when Bro. Inskip led us down to our knees for the baptism, mighty did it come. Scores of seekers were at the altar, and many were able to rest on the promises of a present salvation from sin.

Friday morning we expected to listen to a paper from Dr. D. Steele on the Baptism of the Holy Ghost, but his engagements would not permit him to be present. But God's people are never disappointed. The vacancy was at once filled by several of the brethren, who made brief addresses on the theme.

Bro. McDonald opened the subject by reading a part of the 14th of John's gospel, and the account of the Pentecost. He said: "Christ knew what His Church needed. It was for the advantage of the world that the disciples should be shut in alone in prayer for ten days. The Church has machinery enough. It needs the power from on high. It needs the Baptism of the Holy Ghost that we put our good deeds out of sight, and exalt the Lamb of God."

Bro. Wood said: "I understand the Baptism of the Holy Ghost to be synonymous with purity. The machinery of the Church needs a mighty power to run it. What is needed is a Baptism of the Holy Ghost on Drew Seminary, and Boston University, and Evanston Institute, and on the twelve thousand travelling Methodist ministers, and on the whole Church."

Bro. Browning spoke of his own sweet experience in the Holy Ghost. He thought the recent pastoral address of the Bishops was an earnest expression of their souls that the Church needed a return to the old-fashioned fire.

Dr. Dunn said: "What is the Holy Ghost? What are His relations to us and to the Church? He is more than an agent. He is more than an influence. In every instance where Christ speaks of the Holy Ghost, He speaks of Him as a personality. The promise of the Holy Ghost is that He shall proceed from the Father and the Son. He comes as a Revealer—as a Comforter—as a Sanctifier of the Church.

When He comes into a human heart He comes as a purifier. The Church backslides at the point of refusing to follow the Holy Ghost in His leading to purity. The primary design of the bestowment of the power of the Holy Ghost is, for each receiver to become a witness to the truth. The Holy Ghost is given that we may exalt Jesus Christ."

Bro. Adams spoke of the tenderness of the blessed Holy Ghost. He can be easily grieved. He must have full play in the soul, and must not be interfered with. He spoke also of the progressiveness of the Holy Ghost in the soul. It is a wonderful thing to be a temple of the Holy Ghost. Ralph Waldo Emerson said that "prayer is the mightiest impulse of the universe," but the speaker said, that behind the prayer is the mighty Holy Ghost. An ignorant man under the Spirit's power cannot remain so. He will progress and keep step with God.

Presiding Elder Graves said it seemed to him that we were not sufficiently in the habit of addressing the Holy Ghost in prayer. When we come to the Spirit we come directly to the Fountain. As we honor the Holy Ghost, so does He honor us and honor the Church. In all the appliances of the Church should hold to the idea that this is the dispensation of the Spirit.

At the close of the discussion there was an earnest seeking of the Holy Ghost, and the shouts and praises testified that He had come.

Friday afternoon an essay was read by Rev. I. Simmons on

# THE LIMITATIONS AND POSSIBILITIES OF EVANGELICAL FAITH.

### REV. I. SIMMONS.

What is faith? It is "the assent of the mind to the truth of what is declared by another, resting solely and implicitly on his authority and veracity."

Again, faith is "the assent to the mind of the statement or proposition of another, on the ground of the manifest truth of what he utters."

Faith in its relation to religious truth is twofold; First, it is "the belief in the historic truthfulness of the scripture narrative, and the supernatural origin of its teachings, sometimes called *historical* and *speculative* faith."

Secondly. It is "The belief in the facts and truth of the Scriptures with a practical love of them; especially, that confiding and affectionate belief in the person and work of Christ, which affects the character and life, and makes a man a true Christian." This is called a "*practical, evangelical* or *saving* faith."

According to the Scriptures, Faith is defined "as the *substance* of things hoped for, the evidence of things not seen."

Faith is also used as a concrete term, implying a system of religious belief, especially the system of truth taught by Christ. Hence we are exhorted to "contend earnestly for the *faith* once delivered to the saints."—And to "examine yourselves, whether ye be in the *faith*." Dr. Dwight defines faith to be "That condition of the mind which is called 'trust' or 'confidence' exercised toward the moral character of God, and particularly of the Saviour."

Romaine says: "Faith is to us the evidence of things not

seen, and the ground of our hoping to enjoy them. We believe, upon the authority of God's word, that they are what He describes them to be ; for faith, as a grace of the Spirit, consists in giving credit to what God says. If it be a truth proposed to the understanding, faith relies upon the infallible word. If it be a promise, faith depends upon the arm of God to make it good. And whatever He has promised, faith (when it is as it should be), does not stagger at difficulties, but rests fully persuaded, that what God hath promised, He is able also to perform. Faith looks at the word spoken, and overlooks seeming impossibilities ; *Thus saith the Lord*—that is enough for faith—full of satisfying evidence ; for it knows that to speak and to do are the same thing with an unchangeable God.''

Mr. Wesley says, " Christian faith is not only an assent to the whole gospel of Christ, but also a full reliance upon the blood of Christ : a trust in the merits of His life, death and resurrection ; a recumbency upon Him as our atonement and our life, *as given for us* and *living in us*."

Though the most common of all the theological terms, it is more mystified than they all. Around it have gathered most exciting and protracted word-contests. But I cannot think it was ever intended to be mystified in the fact of its *exercise*, whatever clouds our philosophies might throw over its relations.

Our Saviour spoke to the common people in the simplest language, and when He said, " Have faith in God," they knew He meant, " Have unlimited reliance on God." By His daily unfoldings of sacred truths in the many-sided phases of moral life, they learned that faith

1. Was believing His assertions without further corroboration.

2. That it was believing Him so implicitly that whatever of personal sacrifice to them was involved, they must promptly make it.

3. That it was so believing Him that an entirely new set of purposes and plans of life immediately proceeded to be enforced.

As a result of such faith which, at the first call of the Master, severed them at once from their former selves, they were endowed with new hearts, became as His lambs, leaned on His bosom, learned His inner secrets, and witnessed His glory. But more than this they were taught by Him that to them, through this faith, if it should be unhindered by any unbelief, there should come astounding supernatural powers. Taking the simple statement of Christ by the withered fig-tree, "Have faith in God," and taking His own illustration of it, the removing of a mountain with a grain of faith no larger than a mustard seed, and after you have cut the figure down to the minutest proportions of cold criticism, you will then have, at the smallest end of this divinely-stated power of faith, enough of the supernatural left to perpetuate the most astonishing results in the Christian Church to the end of time.

In discussions on the miracle-working power of faith, it would seem that the idea is entertained that the faith of believers is a wild, capricious power, and subject to no laws. This is far from true. Faith has never been subject to a capricious ruling, either in its limitations or possibilities. Whatever superstition has done, faith is not responsible for. God has built walls heaven-high against both superstition and fanaticism, and has laid rails for the progress of faith which the vandals of unbelief can never tear up. That the mighty products of faith should sometimes be mislabelled fanaticism, and that veneration for promises so much like God, that He puts no limits to them, should sometimes be called superstitious, is simply natural. The province of faith has a vernacular of its own, and no man can understand a faith that goes beyond his own. If a man becomes fanatical by too much believing, he is easily regulated. God has never seemed to fear too much faith, but unbelief, which is fanaticism at white heat, He has severely denounced. No, *faith has its laws*. Its limitations and its possibilities are alike marked out by God.

As a natural defining of my theme, I would assign to the *limitations* of faith, the *subjects* over which faith can have any control. To the *possibilities* of faith I would assign the *extent* to which faith may go in its legitimate field.

1. The limitations. These may be considered as comprising two classes, natural limitations and unnatural limitations.

First, the natural. What can we believe God for? Evidently, the answer must be twofold. The subjects of evangelical faith are primarily and essentially our spiritual conditions. We believe God for justification and regeneration of the penitent soul. "He that believeth shall be saved." "By grace are ye saved through faith." With the soul's conversion, commences the multiplied activities of the Christian life. But not an impulse of the love, not an exercise of the will, not an advance of the nature toward greater light, not a victory of the purpose over the passion that is not an act of faith. The whole history of a soul from the cry for pardon to the crown of supreme victory, is a history of faith.

But if we stop here we have told but half the truth. It is clear from a multitude of cases that might be cited, that the subjects of faith, comprise also the *events* of the believer's life, involving physical changes, exposures and death. Can any one doubt this with the cumulative passages and promises, to this effect, of the New Testament in his hand? I know the universality of the law. I respect its presence and bow to its claims. But does law and law never meet in issues which can only be settled by a concession of the one to the other? Has not faith its laws, and did not Christ recognise this truth, when He brought His disciples to face physical facts without scrip, coat or staff; without organization and without machinery? Most assuredly He did. He made all law. Nothing was made without Him, but while He made the physical law, by whose subversion, a man could be a paralytic, He also made the law by which he could take up his bed and walk. Yes, there are limitations of faith, but you have nothing to do with them. It is for you to ask for whatsoever you desire when you pray, running the "Thy will be done" through the entire length and breadth of the prayer, leaving all the limitations to God. If with sincerity you pray for that you may not have, God will give a substitute that will honor your faith. As sure as the heavens are purer than the earth, as sure as the spirit is superior to matter, as sure as one law has to be subservient to another in high and eternal issues, *so sure* when the law of physics and the law of faith confront each other, must faith have the right of way. I will pay an intelligent deference to all and every law; I will use an enlightened judgment in the analysis of every case to be made a subject of prayer; I will coolly consider the alarmist's warning, lest I put the feathers of fanaticism to the wings of my faith; but then, with all this, I *will*, by the help of the Spirit, *I will* open my New Testament, and with my soul deaf to every sound, I will hear God say, and I will believe it as He speaks, putting an undergirding of omnipotence beneath each word, "All things whatsoever ye shall ask in prayer, believing, ye shall receive." Give me this promise, and this is only one of many, and I will pray, believing up and down the scale of physical subjects, as I do the spiritual.

Secondly, there are *unnatural* limitations to faith. There is first, the tendency to trust to the visible and the near, rather than to the invisible and the distant. If mansions in Central Park were offered for the praying in faith, the avenues of this city would be crowded with kneeling petitioners. If God's gifts were hung out before the eyes, the multitudes would believe for them, but because they are spiritual and invisible, though blessedly real, the faith often flies with drooping wing. That is not faith that leans up against a barrel of flour and prays, "Give us this day our daily bread." It is when the seeking hand scratches the bottom of the empty barrel, and yet the soul doubts not but mightily believes, that the real faith is seen. Believing when there is nothing to rely on but God's word is unlimited faith.

Faith is often limited by our fear of the full answers to our prayers. The rebuke of the formalist, the criticism of the cynic, and the dread of being singular are powerful weights to faith. We cannot tell what God will do with us, and our ignorance hushes the cry of "Thy will be done." *Unlimited faith* sees nothing but God. It mounts above human judgments. Then it is mighty.

2. But the main difficulty is not, what may we pray for, but what are the possibilities of our faith within its legitimate realm?

I doubt if the mass of believers have come to the frontier of their privileges. We live in a bright day, and darkness need cloud no mind. Eighteen centuries of experience are beneath our feet, but have we reached Abraham's faith? Have we soared to the regal heights of his lofty trust? In the presence of his heroic confidence in God's naked word, may we not ask, how far can faith go? It would be bold for me to say, if it were not the Bible language. "All things are possible to him that believeth."

First, what scope has faith in the physical world? Let Williams' work on answers to prayer, and Matthew Hale Smith on the "Marvels of Prayer," and S. H. Platt on his own cure, yea, let the healed cripples, and restored sick and delivered sufferers all answer. There is a host of them, whose characters are too pure, whose intelligence on the subject is too clear to be gainsayed successfully. Men will continue to pray for the sick everywhere, for St. James and the soul's instincts will prompt to it. But why pray and not believe ? We will use the means nature and reason supply, but the pills and the prayers shall work together ; and when the one fails, the other, still pressing its faith-claims to the Father's heart, *shall* prevail. The exceptions will be, not from the imperative restrictions of natural law, but from the will of Him who withholds the pleaded boon to bestow a higher good.

II. What are the possibilities of faith in the spiritual field ? What can we believe God for as it regards our spiritual conditions? Before entering upon the direct answer, let me explain my way. There is a philosophy of faith, but the *possibilities* of faith must be known to each one by his own tests. How far, and for what he can believe God, he alone knows. Two facts seem to be clear : First, that evangelical faith is always in harmony with reason, though often above reasoning. Faith never beats its breast against the iron walls of logic. It is too good logic itself for such folly. If you were to see high enough, you would take notice that faith makes the most perfect syllogisms, that run parallel with the most perfect ones of logic. They are on a higher level, but reason assents when she reaches them. Where reasoning falters,

> " Faith, mighty faith, the promise sees,
>     And looks to that alone ;
>     Laughs at impossibilities,
>     And cries it shall be done."

Faith's grand syllogism is, " God is," " God says," " Therefore." And with this she proves herself to be " the *substance* of things hoped for, and the *evidence* of things not seen."

In the distant reaches of mighty faith, there may be results to the soul, that superficially known, might be denounced as fanaticism. This has occurred through all the history of faith. But examine it closely. Fanaticism rises and falls.

Faith only changes as it grades upward to higher slopes. Fanaticism can give no good reason for itself; faith invites examination, and steadily "keeps step with God."

Another clear fact is, that the believer's faith is the voice within him, which joins with the voice of the Holy Spirit, asserting his spiritual standing. "Without faith it is impossible to please God," whether in coming to Him or staying with Him. Up to the point of believing, we are not accepted by God. We are taught to receive Christ by faith, and that our faith will be its own evidence. Then the Holy Spirit witnessing to our spirits, is a witness to our faith, for if there has been no faith, there is no witness. To this attitude of the soul, as it may be termed, the Holy Ghost comes, and approves, confirms, and intensifies the power that has made it possible for Him to come.

We come now to ask, what are the possibilities of faith in the spiritual realm? I answer, faith is an instrument of supply, adequate to all the necessities of the soul. These necessities are:

1. Deliverance from the guilt of sin. "Being justified by faith, we have peace with God, through our Lord Jesus Christ." We are acquitted, and are without condemnation. This is a necessity generally recognized. Sin shuts out God, and the soul can have peace only through its pardon. The cry of "God be merciful to me a sinner" awakes no controversy. So far all ages in harmony go, but has faith no other power in the soul, than to be present in the tedious round of sinning and repenting, to bring the pardon sought? Surely we have not so misunderstood the Scriptures !

2. Deliverance from the *power* of sin is a crying necessity of the soul. Am I not warranted to believe for this? Am I not on solid rock when I pray that not only may sin's forces be subjugated, but that they may be hurled and kept out, by the power of Him who "came to destroy the works of the

devil!" We cannot be satisfied short of this. It is not enough that we are pardoned convicts, alternately in prison and out of it; we must have, thank God we *can* have the desires, the proclivities, the fiery habit-currents all removed! This is a necessity to complete victory, but God says, "This is the victory that overcometh the world, *even your faith.*" The faith that failed to meet the soul's necessities, would make poor work in overcoming the world. Do not waver, but tell it everywhere, and believe it for yourself now, that you can be delivered from the power of sin. Tell the thief there is something better than being pardoned for theft; it is to be so saved from the tendency to steal, that a thousand purses of uncounted gold would be no temptation to him.

3. Another necessity of the soul is conscious complete harmony with God. We want fellowship with God. This is the most precious work of faith, to lift the soul into sweet repose, thinking, walking and living with God. A truly justified man hungers for this. Sin is odious to him. Earth's pleasures are trifles. He wants God, he was made for God, and but for his want of faith, would abide with God.

Men talk of growth into God by self-culture. Judging by observation of the progress made by what is called growth in grace, it is a tedious process, and wants more time than is allotted to mortal life. Faith is intense culture. It bears the soul into God with astonishing rapidity. It is potent in lifting the soul above its restraints, and clearing away the clouds.

> " Faith lends its realizing light,
> The clouds disperse, the shadows fly ;
> The Invisible appears in sight,
> And God is seen by mortal eye."

Culture is to be desired, but be it remembered, that he who believes God, and stands on the word of promise, gives God an opportunity to make a stupendous spiritual miracle of him. One mighty act of faith, may be a college and library and a course of etiquette all in one, so far as it relates to his being complete in Christ.

The Scriptures furnish the possibilities to faith.—Mark the unlimited expressions the Holy Spirit employs: *"Whatsoever things ye desire* when ye pray, believe that ye receive them and ye shall have them."   Who can define the limits of these underscored words ?   *"All* things, *whatsoever,* ye shall ask in prayer, believing, ye shall receive."   "If ye abide in me and my words abide in you," a condition possible or it would not have been stated, " ye shall ask *what ye will* and  it shall be done unto you."

See also the undefined words in the following passages : " Believe on the Lord Jesus Christ and  thou shalt be *saved."*  Saved from what ?   Saved how far ?   "Come  unto me all ye that labor and are heavy-laden, and I will give you *rest."*  Do those rest who are fighting with inward remains of a carnal nature ?   What is the teaching of these Scripture gems, unless it be that by believing them, the Holy Spirit works the full measure of their meaning, in the soul.   Why should we stagger when it is written that " all  things are  possible to him that believeth ? "

The Scripture *commands* also show the breadth of faith.  " Be ye *holy."*  No interpretation can limit that word up to the acme of human possibility.  It is a state faith must grasp, or it is a mockery.   " Be ye therefore perfect," is an utterance of Christ's that throws a mighty responsibility and blessed prerogative at the feet of our faith.   The radical character and office of other words employed, show  the rock bottom upon which faith for full salvation is to stand.   For instance, the *blood.*  " If we walk in the light, as He is in the light, we have fellowship one with another, and the *blood* of Jesus Christ, His Son, *cleanseth* us from *all* sin."   And again, *"Kept* by the power of God, *through faith,* unto eternal salvation."   Observe the apostle coming from his prayer closet to write his Ephesian brethren for what he had petitioned God in their behalf. Four mighty requests; That they might be mightily strengthened within by the Holy Spirit; that Christ might dwell in their hearts *by faith;* that they might comprehend by faith the infinite love of God that "passeth knowledge;" and that they "might be filled with all the fullness of God." Oh what a prayer for our faith to plead! Another one of his heart burdens has rolled down the ages: "The very God of peace sanctify you wholly; and I pray God your whole spirit, soul and body be preserved blameless unto the coming of our Lord Jesus Christ." "Lord, give us such a faith as this!" But we have more than these isolated passages. The whole drift of the Scriptures, deep and grand, is to show the power of faith in working great results. If you are on the bosom of a vast river, you need no guide boards on the shore to point the direction of its flow. Its never changing current will prove itself, so if you drop yourself any where upon the holy page, the tide will set you toward a perfect life of love through faith in God.

This then is the faith problem. Given a radical evil in the heart, a promise of God of its removal, and the believer's faith, Oh where is the limit? With the promise and the faith, thank God the evil does depart, and the believer is more than conqueror.

And strangely true it is, the faith is the mightiest when the odds seem the greatest against it. When the confirming witnesses are absent and the evidences are yet unrevealed, then, to believe against hope and in the face of many reasons for not believing, is to have the heroic faith of Abraham, Daniel, and Paul. But this is faith's sublimest work. To believe God's word only, when every other utterance is withheld, or made but to oppose, is unmixed faith, and God never failed to honor it.

And grander yet that faith appears when it waits without wavering. God tests faith as well as the virtues of character. He often allows faith to be our only realization of the gift sought: especially is this true of the blessing of perfect love. The writer of this essay waited in a faith-attitude for hours without a witness, but his faith was honored, and the fire came, overwhelming the soul in wave upon wave of heavenly glory, and tingling along the very nerves of his body. Oh the heaven of that moment! If God thus deals with one He may with another. There are diversities of operations. It is ours to consecrate all to God, and then with faith rest on the promise of the cleansing. And now is the moment. As you read these words, as you sit, stand, or kneel, just as you are, give yourself in penitence and consecration and *believe*, oh *believe!* He *will* come, and He will bring the unspeakable peace with Him. "Now unto him who is able to do exceeding abundantly above all that we ask or think, according to the power that worketh in us; unto Him be glory in the Church, by Christ Jesus, throughout all ages, world without end. Amen."

The meeting that followed was one of rare interest and results. With mighty faith many seized the offered grace of full salvation and entered into rest.

The tide of religious fervor was at the flood, when in the evening Bro. Wood preached on "Purity of heart." He said, "This is the most beautiful of all the beatitudes. A justified soul has need of cleansing. In the justified soul the remains of depravity are repressed—kept down. They are matters of consciousness. The work of purification is a work wrought in the soul itself. A man may be as sure that his heart is purified as he is that he needs to be purified. The means of this knowledge are his consciousness, the fruits and the Spirit of God. The blessedness of purity is that it gives intensity to all the faculties exercised in justification. The peace of justification becomes a perfect peace. The love of regeneration becomes a perfect love, having a far wider scope.

10

The blessedness of purity is freedom, vigor of thought, right with God within. The way is delightful. It is liberty. There is also a blessedness in the standpoint which purity gives, which cannot be put into language." The preacher closed with a detailed account of his experience of receiving the blessing. God was in the word. A large number came to the altar to seek the blessedness by faith, and penitents not a few, were among them, seeking for pardon. It was a glorious time, and carried our thoughts back to forest baptisms we remembered, when our eyes beheld the coming of the glory of the Lord.

Still the spirit of consecration and faith increased, and on Saturday A. M. the Lord revealed Himself in a wonderful manner. Many spoke in burning words of His mighty power to save.

The order of the session was an address by Bro. Adams on

## HOLINESS AS IDENTIFIED WITH THE GENERAL INTERESTS OF THE CHURCH.

----

**REV. B. M. ADAMS.**

----

Holiness is as necessary to the existence of a true Church of Christ, as blood is to a human body—it is the life of the Church, or so bound up in the work of the Spirit as to be a part of that life—so essential as to be inseparable from it—as perfume belongs to a true flower; or color to a rainbow. Church organization proceeds on the thought of preparing men to see God, and so they must be holy—all forms of true Church order are arranged around this idea of helping men to be holy—and as constitutional liberty is the central thought of the Government under which we live; so holiness is the ideal around which the government, and order of the evangelical Churches crystallizes. God has always had a true Church in the world, and the experience and practice of holiness, is so identified with it; that no branch of the Church has long existence without it, for a Church without holiness is a body without a soul.

Holiness is the "central idea of Christianity," especially is it of the Methodist Episcopal Church. We declare this to be our mission, to spread Scriptural holiness through these lands; and only as this Church is true to this great mission, may she expect to prosper.

We come to the question, How essential is this identification of Holiness with the general interests of the Church?

The interests of the Church may be classed under two heads: Preservation and Propagation.

I. *Preservation.*

The only thing·God finds worth preserving in this world is His Church. He has demonstrated this in the fact that He destroyed the old world, but saved Noah and his family. He drove the plowshare of fire through Sodom and Gomorrah, while He saved Lot. Jericho was thrown down and sacked, while Rahab and her house were saved. Jerusalem was swept with destruction, while the Church was saved, and He will burn the world up, and all the things therein; but will have the New Jerusalem ready to "come down from God out of heaven," in which to house His Church, for she will never be homeless while God lives. The only thing that makes the Church *worth* saving is her holiness. This is God's thought of her; "the King's daughter is all glorious within." Says Jude, "To them that are sanctified by God the Father, and preserved in Christ Jesus"; and Paul, 1 Thess. v. 23, "The very God of peace sanctify you wholly * * * * your whole spirit, and soul, and body, be preserved blameless unto the coming of our Lord Jesus Christ." Holiness is the quality wrought in the Church, by the Spirit of God. There may be an admirable organization; many Churches have such societies, and manufacturing companies have as good. There may be great influence in the Church, and culture, that may challenge the admiration of the world, but the quality God values is holiness.

*Holiness in the Sanctuary.* The ancient priests wore on their foreheads a ribbon of blue, on which in letters of gold shone " Holiness unto the Lord," to show that the intellect, and governing power of the Church, was to be holy.

*Holiness in the family.* " Every pot in Jerusalem and Judah shall be holiness unto the Lord of Hosts." All the operations of the family are to be carried on under this great idea.

*Holiness in all the movements of the Church.* " The bells of the horses shall be holiness to the Lord." As the on-marching hosts go out to convert the world, the bells that swing from the necks of the horses, that carry the heavenly postillions, shall say at every swing this watchword of the Lord. There are three preservative facts in holiness.

1. *Separation from the world.* The Church must be separate from the world, and as when an epidemic rages in a city, we take our children to the pure country air, or when a fire breaks out we blow up the houses to separate the burning from the unburnt ; so the Church must be separate from the world to keep her in health and save her from destruction —separate not by uniform, though that has a power ; nor by forms of speech, though there is a force behind certain expressions that is not to be denied ; but by holiness in following the plans of God, in Church work, business and pleasure. On an iron ship the compass must be so isolated that it shall not feel the attraction of the iron around it, therefore it is raised up above the deck and away from the affinity that would make the needle unreliable. So the Church must be made so separate from the surrounding world as to be beyond the attraction of it.

2. *Purity*. There may be such a thing as separation without purity. The Mormons are separate from the rest of the world, but no one will claim purity for them. The Communists are separate enough, but no one claims for the societies of our western New York and other States any special purity; so with other so-called separatists, it will not be claimed for many of them, they are pure, because of their isolation from the rest of mankind, but holiness provides purity, as well as separation. Purity by fire, that consumes sin and makes a lofty life possible. A pure atmosphere for the soul is essential to its health and power. The recent discoveries in our cities of the transmission of miasma through the defective waste pipes of our dwellings connected with the sewers, shows that underneath all our elegance of residence and pleasantness of apartments, there may lurk the most fearful diseases, and unless there be purity at the sewer, there can be no health in the family. So unless every department of the Church be holy, her actions will not be pure, either mentally, morally, or spiritually.

3. *Fulness of divine love*. This is the third element, without which the other two are incomplete. The love of God must garrison the soul. We know how in the temperance reform the most efficient ally of drink is want of occupation.

A soldier at Aldershot, in England, to keep himself in employment and so balk the enemy that tempted him to drink, took to sewing, taught himself to sew, and made bed quilts; so that in the hours when off duty he might not have a vacant moment for his enemy's entertainment. A bed quilt, containing thirty-five hundred pieces, was exhibited in Spurgeon's tabernacle in London as his work. This is a law of mind, that it must be occupied with worthy thought, and work to be preserved. Now introduce this mighty factor of the fulness of divine love, and you have a preservative agent that keeps the soul unto eternal life—keeps it in God, and occupied with His work. This occupation of love preserves against the world. As sings the poet in the rapture of this experience—

> " Creatures no more divide my choice,
> I bid them all depart.
> His name, His love, His gracious voice,
> Have fixed my roving heart."

Nothing about God is so terrible as His holiness, and nothing makes His Church so formidable as this quality. Take a single incident from the life of Jacob—God said to him, "Arise, go up to Bethel and dwell there, and make thee an altar unto God, that appeared unto thee when thou fleddest from the face of Esau thy brother." That was holy ground to Jacob: he remembered his vows, made so many years ago and saw the need of purity, both for himself and his household. " Then Jacob said unto his household, and to all that were with him, Put away the strange gods that are among you and be clean, and change your garments, and let us arise and go up to Bethel, and I will there make an altar unto God, who answered me in the day of my distress, and was with me in the way which I went. And they gave unto Jacob all the strange gods which were in their hands, and all the ear-rings which were in their ears, and Jacob hid them under the oak which was by Shechem." And now see the result of this surrender to God, this fullness of obedience to Him—"And they journeyed and the terror of God was upon the cities that were round about them, and they did not pursue after Jacob." The Church at Pentecost was as feeble numerically, and in merely earthly influence, after the baptism as before, but we hear of no molestation on that great occasion when they charged upon the world, and captured three thousand in a day. A Holy Church is worth preserving, and when she is fully occupied by God, she is " terrible as an army with banners."

II. *Propagation.*—A holy Church is the only one worth propagating. Like the trees which are raised in a nursery, the good are kept, the bad cast away as not worth notice, men have enough worthless things now without Churches, worthless from lack of holiness. There is form, ceremony, culture enough, but the thing of value—the quality that makes the apple of the Church desirable—is holiness, and further, a holy Church is the only one that *can* propagate itself.

Churches very unholy do exist; but they are not the authors of a true spiritual seed in the earth. The survival of the fittest is in some aspects very true in respect to Churches. As but for the strong blood coming into cities, the population would soon run out, so but for the little holiness there is in the Churches would they cease to be. They have become extinct in the world, and they will again, if not more holy.

It may be said with increased emphasis, a holy Church is the only one that *can* propagate itself.

Take for application of the principle *revivals of religion*. They can be produced with a very small amount of piety in the Church, yea with none, but they amount to nothing, without holiness as the bottom fact.

*Take the benevolent enterprises of the Church.* The foreign and domestic mission work, if they are weak at the extremity, (and one prominent Church has called a halt along the whole line of its missionary frontier) it is because of weakness at the fountain head. The extremities are inactive, because the heart is weak. Holiness is the incarnation of zeal, and benevolence. A holy Church is one organized and adjusted to do God's work efficiently. God is her power, and the propagation of the cause depends on her perfect adjustment to the force—this adjustment is holiness. In our admirably organized fire department, the steam fire engines always have steam up and so arranged that when the signal is given, the horses are loosed and the engine is flying to the fire in an incredibly short space of time. So the Church of God, has always, and will always find her efficiency in holiness, a perfect adjustment to God. So we may say the success of the Church is in proportion to her holiness. Her work is effective, as she is most fully under the control and inspiration of her Lord. The success of the first stride of the infant Church, shows what relation holiness has to propagation, that success was not the result of organization, or culture, but of holiness. Three thousand were converted in one day. Each fire-baptised disciple counted twenty-five for his day's work. Now counting the population of the world as twelve hundred millions, and take the generally received estimate that there are ten millions of true Christians in the world, if each Christian brought twenty-five souls to Christ in a day, as the result of his or her holy ministry, the prophecy about a nation being "born in a day" would be fulfilled, for ten million fire-anointed saints, would convert two hundred and fifty million in a day, and if each of these converts should re-produce the work of the Pentecost, converting instrumentally twenty-five apiece, the next day would see the world converted with millions to spare. Now take the improvements of the nineteenth century—we can go round the world in eighty days—with the modern improvements in travel, and the means for the dissemination of intelligence, put every one of the ten million nominal Christians, under the holiness of pentecost, and ten years is a very long time to wait for the world's conversion.

The age is one of intense activity, luxury and corruption; nothing can effectually cope with these conditions but a holy Church—give us this and the world is saved.

All hearts were thrilled at the reading of this essay and at the invitation, several bowed and cried unto God for the endowment of power. And it came, blessed be God forever !

After an interesting question meeting in the afternoon, Bro. Wm. Ladd, of the Society of Friends, addressed the Convention, setting forth the relation of his denomination to the doctrine of holiness. For over two hundred years this people have borne aloft the banners of full salvation. Bro. Ladd was requested by unanimous vote, to furnish for publication an article embodying his address.

Bro. McDonald then read an essay on "Errors respecting the doctrine of holiness." It was a masterly review of the errors of Zinzendorf, of salvation by installments, of entire sanctification being sin under control and not sin exterminated, and of imputed holiness

# TITLES in THIS SERIES

geles, 1925), *AROUND THE WORLD BY FAITH, WITH SIX WEEKS IN THE HOLY LAND* (Los Angeles, n. d.), *TWO YEARS MISSION WORK IN EUROPE JUST BEFORE THE WORLD WAR, 1912-14* (Los Angeles, [1926])

6.   Boardman, W. E., *THE HIGHER CHRISTIAN LIFE* (Boston, 1858)

7.   Girvin, E. A., *PHINEAS F. BRESEE: A PRINCE IN ISRAEL* (Kansas City, Mo., [1916])

8.   Brooks, John P., *THE DIVINE CHURCH* (Columbia, Mo., 1891)

9.   *RUSSELL KELSO CARTER ON "FAITH HEALING."* R. Kelso Carter, *THE ATONEMENT FOR SIN AND SICKNESS* (Boston, 1884) *"FAITH HEALING" REVIEWED AFTER TWENTY YEARS* (Boston, 1897)

10.  Daniels, W. H., *DR. CULLIS AND HIS WORK* (Boston, [1885])

11.  *HOLINESS TRACTS DEFENDING THE MINISTRY OF WOMEN.* Luther Lee, *"WOMAN'S RIGHT TO PREACH THE GOSPEL; A SERMON, AT THE ORDINATION OF REV. MISS ANTOINETTE L. BROWN, AT SOUTH BUTLER, WAYNE COUNTY, N. Y., SEPT. 15, 1853"* (Syracuse, 1853) *bound with* B. T. Roberts, *ORDAINING WOMEN* (Rochester, 1891) *bound with* Catherine (Mumford) Booth, *"FEMALE MINISTRY; OR, WOMAN'S RIGHT TO PREACH THE GOSPEL . . ."* (London, n. d.) *bound with* Fannie (McDowell) Hunter, *WOMEN PREACHERS* (Dallas, 1905)

12.  *LATE NINETEENTH CENTURY REVIVALIST TEACHINGS ON THE HOLY SPIRIT.* D. L. Moody, *SECRET POWER OR THE SECRET OF SUCCESS IN CHRISTIAN LIFE AND*

WORK (New York, [1881]) *bound with* J. Wilbur Chapman, *RECEIVED YE THE HOLY GHOST?* (New York, [1894]) *bound with* R. A. Torrey, *THE BAPTISM WITH THE HOLY SPIRIT* (New York, 1895 & 1897)

**13.** SEVEN "JESUS ONLY" TRACTS. Andrew D. Urshan, *THE DOCTRINE OF THE NEW BIRTH, OR, THE PERFECT WAY TO ETERNAL LIFE* (Cochrane, Wis., 1921) *bound with* Andrew Urshan, *THE ALMIGHTY GOD IN THE LORD JESUS CHRIST* (Los Angeles, 1919) *bound with* Frank J. Ewart, *THE REVELATION OF JESUS CHRIST* (St. Louis, n. d.) *bound with* G. T. Haywood, *THE BIRTH OF THE SPIRIT IN THE DAYS OF THE APOSTLES* (Indianapolis, n. d.) *DIVINE NAMES AND TITLES OF JEHOVAH* (Indianapolis, n. d.) *THE FINEST OF THE WHEAT* (Indianapolis, n. d.) *THE VICTIM OF THE FLAMING SWORD* (Indianapolis, n. d.)

**14.** THREE EARLY PENTECOSTAL TRACTS. D. Wesley Myland, *THE LATTER RAIN COVENANT AND PENTECOSTAL POWER* (Chicago, 1910) *bound with* G. F. Taylor, *THE SPIRIT AND THE BRIDE* (n. p., [1907?]) *bound with* B. F. Laurence, *THE APOSTOLIC FAITH RESTORED* (St. Louis, 1916)

**15.** Fairchild, James H., *OBERLIN: THE COLONY AND THE COLLEGE, 1833-1883* (Oberlin, 1883)

**16.** Figgis, John B., *KESWICK FROM WITHIN* (London, [1914])

**17.** Finney, Charles G., *LECTURES TO PROFESSING CHRISTIANS* (New York, 1837)

**18.** Fleisch, Paul, *DIE MODERNE GEMEINSCHAFTSBEWEGUNG IN DEUTSCHLAND* (Leipzig, 1912)

19. SIX TRACTS BY W. B. GODBEY. *SPIRITUAL GIFTS AND GRACES* (Cincinnati, [1895]) *THE RETURN OF JESUS* (Cincinnati, [1899?]) *WORK OF THE HOLY SPIRIT* (Louisville, [1902]) *CHURCH—BRIDE—KINGDOM* (Cincinnati, [1905]) *DIVINE HEALING* (Greensboro, [1909]) *TONGUE MOVEMENT, SATANIC* (Zarephath, N. J., 1918)

20. Gordon, Earnest B., *ADONIRAM JUDSON GORDON* (New York, [1896])

21. Hills, A. M., *HOLINESS AND POWER FOR THE CHURCH AND THE MINISTRY* (Cincinnati, [1897])

22. Horner, Ralph C., *FROM THE ALTAR TO THE UPPER ROOM* (Toronto, [1891])

23. McDonald, William and John E. Searles, *THE LIFE OF REV. JOHN S. INSKIP* (Boston, [1885])

24. LaBerge, Agnes N. O., *WHAT GOD HATH WROUGHT* (Chicago, n. d.)

25. Lee, Luther, *AUTOBIOGRAPHY OF THE REV. LUTHER LEE* (New York, 1882)

26. McLean, A. and J. W. Easton, *PENUEL; OR, FACE TO FACE WITH GOD* (New York, 1869)

27. McPherson, Aimee Semple, *THIS IS THAT: PERSONAL EXPERIENCES SERMONS AND WRITINGS* (Los Angeles, [1919])

28. Mahan, Asa, *OUT OF DARKNESS INTO LIGHT* (London, 1877)

29. THE LIFE AND TEACHING OF CARRIE JUDD MONTGOMERY Carrie Judd Montgomery, *"UNDER HIS WINGS": THE STORY OF MY LIFE* (Oakland,

[1936]) Carrie F. Judd, THE PRAYER OF FAITH (New York, 1880)

30. THE DEVOTIONAL WRITINGS OF PHOEBE PALMER Phoebe Palmer, THE WAY OF HOLINESS (52nd ed., New York, 1867) FAITH AND ITS EFFECTS (27th ed., New York, n. d., orig. pub. 1854)

31. Wheatley, Richard, THE LIFE AND LETTERS OF MRS. PHOEBE PALMER (New York, 1881)

32. Palmer, Phoebe, ed., PIONEER EXPERIENCES (New York, 1868)

33. Palmer, Phoebe, THE PROMISE OF THE FATHER (Boston, 1859)

34. Pardington, G. P., TWENTY-FIVE WONDERFUL YEARS, 1889-1914: A POPULAR SKETCH OF THE CHRISTIAN AND MISSIONARY ALLIANCE (New York, [1914])

35. Parham, Sarah E., THE LIFE OF CHARLES F. PARHAM, FOUNDER OF THE APOSTOLIC FAITH MOVEMENT (Joplin, [1930])

36. THE SERMONS OF CHARLES F. PARHAM. Charles F. Parham, A VOICE CRYING IN THE WILDERNESS (4th ed., Baxter Springs, Kan., 1944, orig. pub. 1902) THE EVERLASTING GOSPEL (n.p., n.d., orig. pub. 1911)

37. Pierson, Arthur Tappan, FORWARD MOVEMENTS OF THE LAST HALF CENTURY (New York, 1905)

38. PROCEEDINGS OF HOLINESS CONFERENCES, HELD AT CINCINNATI, NOVEMBER 26TH, 1877, AND AT NEW YORK, DECEMBER 17TH, 1877 (Philadelphia, 1878)

39. RECORD OF THE CONVENTION FOR THE PROMOTION OF

*Scriptural Holiness Held at Brighton, May 29th, to June 7th, 1875* (Brighton, [1896?])

**40.** Rees, Seth Cook, *Miracles in the Slums* (Chicago, [1905?])

**41.** Roberts, B. T., *Why Another Sect* (Rochester, 1879)

**42.** Shaw, S. B., ed., *Echoes of the General Holiness Assembly* (Chicago, [1901])

**43.** *The Devotional Writings of Robert Pearsall Smith and Hannah Whitall Smith.* [R]obert [P]earsall [S]mith, *Holiness Through Faith: Light on the Way of Holiness* (New York, [1870]) [H]annah [W]hitall [S]mith, *The Christian's Secret of a Happy Life*, (Boston and Chicago, [1885])

**44.** [S]mith, [H]annah [W]hitall, *The Unselfishness of God and How I Discovered It* (New York, [1903])

**45.** Steele, Daniel, *A Substitute for Holiness; or, Antinomianism Revived* (Chicago and Boston, [1899])

**46.** Tomlinson, A. J., *The Last Great Conflict* (Cleveland, 1913)

**47.** Upham, Thomas C., *The Life of Faith* (Boston, 1845)

**48.** Washburn, Josephine M., *History and Reminiscences of the Holiness Church Work in Southern California and Arizona* (South Pasadena, [1912?])